LEO RASTOGI, PhD

Life is Good

Embracing life's meaning on the
journey to happiness and fulfillment

This is book is dedicated to
Bhante Vimalaramsi Mahathera,
the monk who gave me the gift of the smile!

ACKNOWLEDGEMENTS

A book about happiness, meaning, and purpose and fulfillment cannot but have shades of learning from personal life, with moments shared with those closest with you. Not just your family but countless others who have walked with you, not only in celebrations but also in moments not so pleasant although still a great source of learning. I only wish I could credit them all. I hope my gratitude expressed in my mediations reaches them. This book is special for me in the sense that is deeply personal, and a little biographical too.

I will begin with acknowledging my parents Dr. A.P Rastogi and Dr. Rekha Rastogi, for they modeled for me a life lived with fulfillment. Dr. Richa, for deep conversations we have shared, many of which found their way into this book. My sister, Nirjhara for being a philosophical sounding board since you were literally learning to speak, your presence makes me connect with happiest (sibling) moments of childhood we spent together growing up.

A special shout out to Vineet, for being perhaps the most significant co-traveler in my foundational years, and a an echo chamber for my formative ideas around meaning and purpose, and supporting me when I needed to make major transitions.

I want to extend a special thanks to Javi and Charlie for embodying the message of this book, and being the persistent request that I write it: this book exists literally because you asked for it. My wonderful coworkers at ayam™, especially Anna, for support in converting this book into a transformative course we co-teach.

I am blessed to have wonderful friends and colleagues who have been a source of support, ideas, and shared moments featured as my personal anecdotes in the books - Ale, Charlie, Suzanne, Tono, Rodrigo Alice, Karol, Pepy – thank you.

In closing, I want to thank my editorial and design team, Wendi & Gillian. Thank you for your editorial and research support, Ceci for making the book look beautiful – especially twice! If it weren't for you all, this book would never have seen the light of day!

CONTENT

SECTION 1
Welcome   13

    CHAPTER 1
    Introduction   15

    CHAPTER 2
    Real Life and the Other   19

SECTION 2
Decoding the Enigma of Happiness   33

    CHAPTER 3
    The History of Happiness   35

    CHAPTER 4
    The Hedonic Treadmill of Modern Life   49

    CHAPTER 5
    Digitally Disrupted Generations   63

    CHAPTER 6
    The Six Levels of Happiness   77

    CHAPTER 7
    The Journey from Happiness to Fulfillment   89

SECTION 3
Nurturing the Seeds   103

    CHAPTER 8
    Gratitude   105

    CHAPTER 9
    Goodwill and the Will to Do Good   117

CHAPTER 10
Love and Compassion 129

CHAPTER 11
Forgiveness and Self-Healing 139

CHAPTER 12
Family, Friends, and Faith 151

CHAPTER 13
Conscious Meaning-Making 161

CHAPTER 14
Nurturing Purpose, Transcending
Achievement, Unfolding Actualization 173

CHAPTER 15
Living Your Greatest Life:
Past, Present, and Future 185

CHAPTER 16
Creating a WOW Workplace 195

SECTION 4
Moving Forward 207

CHAPTER 17
Living the Everyday Life:
The Paradigm of Self-Care and Well-Being 209

CHAPTER 18
A Final Inquiry:
Who Am I and Where To Go From Here? 219

Life is Good

Conversations about
Happiness, Joy and Fulfillment

SECTION 1

Welcome

What does it mean to be happy? What does it mean –
and what does it take – to live a life that truly fulfills us?
How can we experience fulfillment in all dimensions of
our life, from work to home and in the spaces between?
These questions (and many more) are what we will set
out to explore in this book. Welcome to the journey.

CHAPTER 1

Introduction

Why This Book?

The subject of the meaning of life has always intrigued me. Over the years, I have approached this subject from many lenses, including that of spirituality, philosophy, psychology, and faith, to name but a few. One theme that I kept coming across in my conversations with everyone ranging from priest to scientist were the same subjects of happiness and fulfillment. I quickly realized that these words meant something completely different to different people and at different stages of life. This led me to take the opportunity to have a series of conversations in different contexts – corporate workplace well-being, spiritual retreats, academic research conferences – about what it meant to live a happy and fulfilled life.

While very spirited, these conversations almost always included some inquiries that would deepen the dialogues and speculation on certain practices that would actually deepen the embodiment. Soon enough, I was asked by my colleagues at **ayam** to design a program on the theme, which would be offered as a public retreat. I then looked around for a book/ resource material that I could offer to participants as a pre or post-read. There are hundreds of books written from different lenses, ranging from Buddhist thought and positive psychology to some empirical research and philosophically complex works. Despite this, I failed to find a book that would allow readers from different orientations to approach this subject as a series of conversations and inquiries so they can draw their own conclusions.

This was important to me because I truly believe that every human being is unique and their experience of being alive is unique. Hence, I don't subscribe to a "rule book" approach to something as subtle, profound, and personal as happiness and fulfillment. And as I have done previously, on realizing that *if there is no such book, then you have to write one because, as a teacher, that's your only choice."* Hence, this book. I have not written it to fall within the self-help genre or as a DIY tool book. Rather, it is an immersive conversational journey that allows you to enquire into the various topics related to the subject.

You can use it to try some simple practices, consolidate your insights and experience into your own life philosophy, and apply that to nurture your own unique sense of happiness. This book is meant to be read, thought about, practiced, and then integrated as you chose in your life!

What Will We Cover?

We will begin our journey by taking a look at what life really is. What were we taught to aim for in life and does this align with what we truly yearn for? Furthermore, how does the life we long for compare with the one we are actually living? We'll also dive into the history of happiness, taking a look at various perspectives on happiness across time and culture.

Next, we will dive into the conditions of this modern life (and how those conditions support or hinder happiness) before exploring what happiness really means in greater depth. Happiness, as most of us can sense, comes in different shades or flavors. How do we, for instance, differentiate between the happiness that arises when we achieve a goal at work and the joy that comes from experiencing a deeper sense of purpose within our community? We will consider how we might journey across the gradient of varying flavors of happiness, moving closer to deep fulfillment.

Once we have a good sense of what we are working towards, we will explore various seeds of positive emotion, which fuel our wellbeing. We will take a look at the act of meaning making, how to nurture a sense of purpose, how the past and future mingle with the present, and what it takes to create a workplace that inspires and nourishes.

As we close the book, we will venture into what it means to take care of ourselves – to nurture our well-being – and then we'll inquire: Where do we go from here? You will be invited to get curious about how you can take the insights that arise from this book and work them into your lived experience.

How to Use This Book

I offer this book to you not as a self-help manual. It is not designed to quickly 'fix' or to 'solve' any challenges in your life and it will not tell you what to do. It is not deeply psychological nor is it a philosophical 'prescription' about how to lead a great life. Instead, this is an inquiry. It will provide you with enough information to trigger questions and curiosities that will lead to your own insights.

Happiness is, after all, not a recipe. It is more of an art, which does not come with a clear-cut rulebook. Furthermore, each one of us has our own path to take, which is why happiness prescriptions typically do not work. As you sit with this book and the insights that arise, you will be able to integrate some of them, which will shift your perspective of life along with your experience of it.

This book will invite you to think in ways that you might not typically think. It does not offer you a 'right way' to think and you may disagree with some of what you read. This is completely fine – you are free to take what works for you and leave the rest. In fact, both agreement and disagreement can lead to deeper layers of inquiry, so long as we engage thoughtfully with the questions and ideas put forth.

Above all, this book is here to help you re-examine assumptions you have about your life and about life in general. It will invite you to explore how you are shaping your life and how you've arrived at the place you are at now. My intention is that you walk away with a sense of agency, becoming a more conscious creator of the one life you are leading. After all, this is *your* life. What do you want to make of it?

CHAPTER 2

Real Life and the Other

"Happiness is not something ready-made.
It comes from your own actions."
Dalai Lama

For most of us, the education we received in our younger years focused primarily on success, with happiness being an afterthought – if discussed at all. Many were raised in a system (*growing up Indian, I certainly was*) that wanted us to excel in math, English, and science, and did little to educate us on how to nurture our sense of happiness, our sense of wholeness, and our holistic well-being. It was never a subject in school or university, much less so a learning objective of the education system.

Yet, if you ask most parents what they want for their children, the answer is a resounding, "happiness and well-being!" Typically, parents also want their children to succeed academically or professionally, but happiness is the wish that comes from the heart. It is my deepest wish.

This came home to me so movingly later in life when I met my friend Christopher and saw the great work he has been doing to help co-create a school of the future, a project that I went on to invest in and collaborate closely with.

And, of course, this discussion is not limited to childhood, I remember from my corporate years — from research labs in Silicon Valley to board rooms – rarely, if ever, does happiness come up amongst the countless discussions on 'stock options', 'retirement accounts', 'financial independence', etc., etc.

As a result of this divide, many of us have developed cognitive dissonance between what we really want and the life that we are actually creating. We have focused much of our energy on what we *should* want or what we *thought* we wanted. But as time goes on, we realize that there are dreams, values, and visions left unattended to. And often, we realize that we are living two lives; one that is our reality and one that is imaginary – the perfect one that we are waiting for to begin.

Living Two Lives

Despite what the name may suggest, the double life we might find ourselves leading is not about secrets, or hiding actions and behaviors from those that we love. Rather, it is about physically living this life 'here' and mentally escaping to another one 'there' – in our imagination or *wishdom*. Our real life is tangible whereas our 'other life' is ideal and perpetually lying in the future. The life that is tangible involves what we're *actually* doing for work, how we *actually* spend our days and the *actual* nature of our relationships. As we go through the motions of real life, we may simultaneously escape to the one in our mind – to the job we wish we had, to the things we wish we were doing, and to the types of relationships, conversations, and environments we wish to engage in.

Most of us are familiar with that experience of reading a full page of a book and upon reaching the bottom, realizing we can't recall what we've just read. We might have been busy thinking about a conversation that took place earlier in the day or worrying about a decision we have to make in the days ahead. In the same way, we can go through the motions of real life without actually being there, almost waiting for our real life to begin someday.

This imagined life we escape to typically involves a dream we hold of the future. For instance, we might envision the happiness we believe we'll attain when we are able to buy the house of our dreams or when we reach the top rung of the corporate ladder we've been climbing.

There can also be an element of the past in our 'other life' – a holding onto grudges or a waiting for an apology that may never come. We might secretly be holding onto remnants of childhood dreams, waiting for the day when the conditions will be right to go after them. Often, we think that we can turn the imaginary life of our dreams into reality once a certain level of financial stability has been reached – and yet we often come to see that our sense of 'stability' is an elusive, ever-shifting goal post. We never truly 'get there' and all the while happiness has been put on hold.

It is also worth noting that, although we have this concept of two lives – the real and the imagined – there is another perspective that suggests we live three lives in one. In addition to our lived reality and the life we envision for ourselves, there is also the life that others *think* we are living, or that we are suggesting we live. We often present a particular image to the world based on what we think is expected of us or what our culture and community values. When this does not align with the truth of who we are, it creates further unease and disharmony.

Ultimately, happiness, wholeness, or well-being can only be experienced in real life, and only when our thoughts, actions, and projections are in alignment with our truest yearnings. So long as we are chasing some idealized image in the hamster wheel of our mind, or so long as we are presenting an image to the world that is not in alignment with our truth, we will not experience the joy and fulfillment that we long for. So how do we make the transition to greater well-being? We must begin by examining what constitutes our real life. That brings us to the million-dollar question of just *how do we get a sense of what is 'real' in our lives?*

What Is In Your Calendar?

Real life is what is on our calendar. It represents what we are *actually* doing – how we are *actually* spending our time. Each square or series of lines in our calendar represents what takes place on a given day. Though we might not write everything down, what we *do* write down acts as a snapshot of what we are prioritizing. Additionally, it can provide insights into *how* we are engaging with the content of our life.

Our calendar can quickly fill with the practicalities of life. We often focus on what *needs* to get done before penning in what we *desire* to do. There are many reasons for this, from a demanding work schedule to childhood conditioning that provided us with more tools on how to succeed professionally and financially than spiritually and emotionally. Regardless of the reason, if our calendar does not represent the fullness of who we are, something needs to shift.

To make that shift – to experience more of what it means to be alive – we have two opportunities. The first opportunity is to change the actual content of what we are doing. What isn't in our calendar that we want to be in our calendar? Is there too much of something and not enough of another thing? This is the first line of inquiry.

The second is to shift our relationship to whatever it is that we do. Are the contents of our calendar task-oriented or do they imbue a sense of joy, purpose, and contentment? Are we meeting the activities of each day with a sense of openness, acceptance, and/or curiosity?

To get a better idea of how this works in a practical sense, let's take a look at an example. The following is Daniel's schedule for Monday:

- 20-minute meeting with the boss
- Performance reviews for Katie, Sherry, and Jay
- Finish filing business receipts
- Pick up kids from the babysitter before heading home
- Call mom

Without overanalyzing this very simple example, what is the overall energy you pick up from Daniel's schedule? Can you get a sense of the quality of Daniel's day?

It might be hard to tell without knowing more about Daniel, but what if we were to find out that Daniel loves being active and the outdoors? He works in a digital agency, for the most part enjoys his job, but he often feels there is little energy left at the end of the day to tend to the needs of his kids and partner, who he loves very much.

Daniel's calendar shows no signs of any plans to connect with the things that he loves – being active, the outdoors, his partner, or his children. Rather, the focal point of his day is what happens at work. If he were to adjust his calendar to schedule in time for the things that nourish him, his Monday might look like this:

- 20-minute meeting with the boss
- Performance reviews for Katie, Sherry, and Jay
- 5-minute meditation at lunch
- Finish filing business receipts
- Leave work by 5 pm latest

- Pick up kids from the babysitter before heading home
- Cook dinner with Zoe
- Take a walk to the beach with Zoe, Sam, and Mikaela
- Call mom

Making a conscious decision to include more of what you love in your calendar is a simple shift that has a big impact on the contents of your day. Home life, creative life, spiritual life, or any other aspect of life that is important to you gets prioritized in the same way that work life does.

In addition to shifting the content of one's calendar, we can also address the way in which we are relating to our daily tasks. In fact, we might even shift the word 'task' to something that imbues a different energy. If we think about the contents of our day as 'commitments' or 'accomplishments' instead, we begin to establish a new relationship with what we are doing, even with the aspects of our day that are less enjoyable.

Coming back to Daniel's calendar, shifting the lens from 'tasks' to 'commitments and accomplishments', his schedule for Monday might look like this:

- 20-minute meeting with Sandra to gain more clarity and insight
- Performance reviews for Katie, Sherry, and Jay to show appreciation and support their growth
- 5-minute meditation at lunch to increase peace and presence
- Get organized by filing the last of the business receipts
- Commit to heading back home by 5 pm
- Pick up my wonderful children Sam and Mikaela from Patsy's house
- Cook a delicious and nutritious meal with Zoe (salmon tacos and fresh salad!)
- Take a walk to the beach with Zoe, Sam, and Mikaela (bring the football!)
- Call Mom to express my love and care for her

Now, come back to the questions posed previously. What is the overall energy you pick up from Daniel's new schedule? What qualities are embedded within the content of his day?

Practically speaking, not a lot changed. In another way, his schedule looks very different. Depending on who we are and what we are currently experiencing in life, adaptations to our current calendar will look different for each of us. The key here rests in the truth that we all have the power to begin making changes not only to the content of our calendar but to how we show up for it.

"There is no way to happiness, happiness is the way."
Unknown

The Bridge to the Other

Examining and making shifts to the content of our lives is the first step in bridging the gap between our real life and the one we imagine for ourselves. It may seem easier said than done but the reality is that each day – each moment, for that matter – provides us with an opportunity to do things differently. We will continue to need to pay the bills and there are certain challenges of life that we cannot escape, but how do we wish to really show up for our lives? What are the deeper visions and values we wish to live in accordance with?

We aren't always sure of how to begin living our ideal or perfect life and there can be a lot of fear, uncertainty, or confusion around doing so. It is helpful to remember that you don't need all the answers now. You can simply begin with the question:

What kind of life do I wish to craft?

Crossing the bridge into a life that brings us more happiness and fulfillment means delving deeper into our most authentic dreams, values, and visions. As human beings, our desires can be complex and multi-faceted, even contradictory. What do we do then? The key is in moving beneath our surface-level desires to start discovering what has the *deepest* meaning for us. What nourishes us more holistically than the limited notions of success that we've been taught to chase?

Your dreams, values, and visions will change over time, so you don't need to worry about finding what will last you your lifetime. Nothing lasts a full lifetime and so it is okay – and even wise – to simply begin where we are. This knowledge can also help us to realize that previous visions of success may have been valid for a time but have since expired. This can help us to view our previous successes and achievements not as bad or wrong but as a necessary part of our journey, just as the transition that rests before us is necessary for this next period of time in our lives.

This transition into greater fulfillment often requires a letting go – a letting go of our attachment to certain outcomes we started working towards long ago. For myself, this realization came after 15 years spent in a career as a corporate CEO. I came to see that if I wanted to have the *lived* experience of being a teacher (not the imagined experience), I could not carry my previous financial or personal goals into the future. The new chapter I was stepping into meant relinquishing these attachments while trusting that my new, heart-centered visions would be enough to carry me.

As you consider ways in which you can bridge the gap and step into a new experience of life, all sorts of inner resistance may arise. You might notice thoughts along the lines of:

- I can't just leave my job. I have a family to support.

- I don't know what would bring me a greater sense of fulfillment.

- I could lose friends or other loved ones if I change things up.

- It's too risky / I'm too scared / I can't do it.

First of all, if fear is there, let it be there but try to recognize that the stories of fear are not fact. You *can* take steps in the direction of a life that is in greater alignment with who you are deep down. Relationships might change, but the closer you stay to your values and to your deepest personal truth, the easier it will be to navigate these changes.

Furthermore, you do not need to leave your job. You do not need to make any specific drastic changes. Your journey is your own and you get to decide what works best for you at this moment. With that said, there are always steps you can take. Rather than waiting for the perfect time to leap, start with consecutive baby steps in the direction of your dreams and you'll be surprised at where you find yourself a year from now.

The Allure of the Illusion

It is important to consider that the illusory world we hold in our minds can capture the interest of both our desire to align with our true nature *and* any yearning we might have to avoid challenges past or present. In other words, moving towards our idealized life can be either unifying and wholesome or it can be used as a form of escape, another distraction from living a full, integrated life.

The yearning to escape an unsatisfactory or overwhelming experience of life is natural. Just like a pendulum, our instinct might be to move just as far in the opposite direction of the one we were previously moving in. For example, a high-performing, burned-out CEO of a company might decide one afternoon to leave it all – to use the financial stability that has been earned to fly to a tropical oasis and fully renounce the life left behind.

While doing so is not 'wrong' per se, we have to be mindful that going with the full swing of the pendulum in *any* direction will likely see us reverting to the polar opposite at some point in the future. If we have not taken a close, honest look at the issues we are facing and if we use an idealized image of how life should be as an escape from 'real life', our new circumstances will only grant us temporary, superficial happiness. For true fulfillment, we need to go deeper and craft a life that is balanced and sustainable.

We can also see this yearning to escape manifest in the tendency to take formal retreats when life becomes 'too much'. While there is nothing wrong with taking a retreat when our inner life begs for it, this approach is not sustainable. True bridging of the gap between our real life and our imagined life involves *living* our values, our peace, and our purpose in a more integrated way.

While meditation, yoga, and other self-care practices might be viewed as medication to some, please do not use these techniques in this way. Escaping to paradise or getting a quick fix of peace on a long-weekend retreat is not a substitute for a good life. To experience the life we most authentically long for, we must be willing to engage in our life – to figure out ways to embody our values and our vision on a day-to-day basis.

The challenges we face now are an opportunity to take a closer look at our life and to learn more about what we really need for greater well-being. Rather than reacting by running away in one form or another, we are called during times of difficulty to respond with care and curiosity. Whatever shows up on our path provides us with clues as to what we need (or don't need) to cultivate a great life for ourselves.

One way to take a closer look at whether our efforts to make change are motivated by a yearning to escape versus a desire to move closer to our highest personal truth is to consider which of the two following paradigms our efforts fall into:

1. Coping/Survival Skills

2. Life Tools

Are the steps we are planning to take motivated by a desire to cope (i.e. reduce negative experience) or to grow (i.e. increase positive experience)? It is natural to want to reduce difficult experiences, and we can certainly work towards this. But for a great life, we need to simultaneously ask ourselves what we want to create or cultivate. Discovering life tools that help to maximize our life experience is how we move from surviving to thriving.

Sometimes, we hear things measured in terms of their MA – the 'minimum acceptable'. For example: What is the 'minimum acceptable' rate of return? What is the 'minimum acceptable' diet for infants and young children? Even if unconsciously, we tend to view well-being in the same terms, considering what our minimum acceptable experience of life would be. It could be a life without anxiety, a life without depression, or a life where we feel as though things are okay (enough).

What if we were to call our MA our 'maximum achievable' instead? What if we could start aiming for our highest life experience potential? By shifting our lens in this way, we create space for more than 'just okay'. We acknowledge that a great life is not just about minimizing what isn't working but also about maximizing what we want more of, be it love, gratitude, acceptance, meaning, purpose, or something else.

Again, this is a two-fold approach. It involves addressing the content of our lives as well as the context – how we approach whatever life puts in front of us. The allure of the illusion often comes from the misconception that we can escape the difficulties of life if we just get the content right. But the reality is that no matter how well we craft the details of our life, fulfillment and joy will not come if we do not know how to approach hardships. As Jon Kabat-Zinn wrote in his book *Wherever You Go, There You Are*:

> *"You can't stop the waves, but you can learn to surf."*

📓 Journal Exercise: Pause for Reflection

We can conceptualize this idea of making change and bridging the gap between real life and the other, but the real work requires that we look within. Turning inward calls for curiosity, patience, and self-compassion as it is not always easy to acknowledge what isn't working in our lives and what we're missing. As you move through the following reflection questions, be sure to harness these qualities. Write your answers down in a journal and review them often.

Know that there is no place you are supposed to be right now other than where you are. Only by accepting this moment of our real life for what it is do we find the strength to honor wherever we wish to go.

1. Take out your calendar and scan through the content written in it. If you have not kept an up-to-date calendar lately, take some time to write out what's on your agenda in the coming days. Write it out as you naturally would without trying to shape it in any particular 'desirable' way.

2. After taking in the contents of your calendar as it stands, how satisfied are you with what constitutes your life? Is it dissatisfactory? Satisfactory? Is it more than satisfactory? You might decide to rate what sits in your calendar on a satisfaction scale from 1 to 10.

3. What would a great life look like to you? Consider your passions, your values, your dreams, and your visions as you answer this.

4. How much of your life would you change if you had only one year to live? What changes would you make?

5. With all of the above inquiries in mind, how can you adjust the content of your calendar for this week, month, or year?

6. How can you adjust the way that you relate to what is on your calendar? If certain content cannot be changed in the short-term, how can you shift your relationship to it for the time being?

My Drives with Sonja

When I was a young tech entrepreneur, I chanced upon a business association that soon became a friendship with a very mercurial and wonderful person I am choosing to call Sonja. He was a retired military officer who had decided to build a career in the tech space and co-founded a company with another young professional. Our respective firms were collaborating on a sizable project that required me to travel with him to client sites often, including long road journeys. As I spent more time with him, I realized a very curious pattern. He would often tell wonderful takes of his exploits as an army officer and how he challenged the status quo, etc., mostly making him out to be a superbly competent officer rising fast in the armed forces. It always intrigued me that if his career in such a noble profession was going so well, why he resigned at an early age – let's say early 30s – without attaining even a pensionable rank. A couple of times I approached the subject with him, but he evaded any answers and quickly moved on to other topics.

Soon enough, I also noticed him telling me wonderful stories of his successful career as a stock trader and I had the same curiosity – why would he quit if he was so successful? And in this case, I was further intrigued by the lack of any signs of financial success in his life from his stock trader career. And there were yet more stories of other great achievements that also did not seem to fit/reflect in the current realities of his life. Being the naïve 22 year old I was, I chalked it up to "fanciful bragging" and didn't think much about it.

Over the years and as our friendship grew, he began to confide in me about his plans for a future nationwide retail network he had been planning to execute that his children could run (note, his children were currently 3- and 5-year-old) and he could retire to a farmhouse in the hills. And all this while I noticed his day-to-day cash struggles in keeping his business afloat. He also discussed his future IPO plans with me in the same year when his business clocked less than 2 million and did not have any profit, and he didn't seem to have a plan of any kind to grow his business. But he spoke of a future IPO almost as if it was a done deal.

As time passed, I moved on to other things and we kept in touch occasionally, sometimes meeting over lunch or dinner. Without fail, every time I saw him, he had a great new story to tell about how in the next year his plan was all going to come together. By this time, I had some more life experience, so I always wished him well and sincerely offered to help in any way he needed (in 15 years of knowing him, he never asked).

Then, we had a call once about how he had decided that "IPO was too much work" (at this time his revenues had steadily declined almost to a trickle) and he was going to venture into real estate to build office towers in Dubai – a country he had never visited before. I must admit that at this point, I was more interested in enquiring about his health and the well-being of his family and that was the focus of our conversation. A couple of months later I heard from a common friend that he had a massive heart attack while driving and could not be revived.

I was both shocked and saddened to hear of the news. He had sounded so upbeat just a couple of months ago that a part of me wished I had talked to him longer that day. As mercurial as he was, I was fond of him as a friend. A few days later, as I was driving on a route I had previously driven many times with him, the student of human nature in me could not help but muse – were his *always new plans* a sign of his optimistic attitude to life or his never say die spirit? Or were they a reflection of his escaping/living often enough in an imaginary life he was building and, if so, was he aware of this?

Now, I will never know and it does not matter. As a friend, he is truly missed. But the question in itself is one worth reflecting on for each one of us as it pertains to our life. Which of the three lives we discussed in the chapter do we spend our most time in, and how checked-in we are with our real lives?

SECTION 2

Decoding the Enigma of Happiness

Happiness is a mystery. It is a word that is used a lot but one that is hard to define. It is something each one of us aspires to experience more integrally but we don't often know how to go about it. Furthermore, if you could gather people from across the globe (and even from across time) into a single room to ask them what they thought happiness to be, you would likely get a whole range of answers.

Additionally, happiness in the modern world can be complex. With a variety of pleasure-inducing items and activities available at our fingertips, we might experience more confusion about what happiness really entails than our ancestors did. It is not uncommon in this modern age to become caught on a treadmill of temporary pleasures, but how do we go deeper? How do we experience broader layers of what happiness might be, and what are those layers that await us? We will explore all of this and more in this section.

CHAPTER 3

The History of Happiness

"Happiness has always been an elusive concept – difficult to define, and even more difficult to measure. But throughout history, people have pursued happiness with great fervor, and many have believed that it is not only a desirable goal but a fundamental human right."
Gretchen Rubin

When people talk about happiness, we can't assume or be sure we know what they are referring to. Despite it sometimes feeling simple or obvious, the concept is complex since happiness has meant different things at different times and across different cultures. Happiness cannot be quantified; it is a quality that we know only through experience and, as such, can be difficult to put into words.

Yet, if we are to explore happiness in this book, we need to come to some basic understanding of what we are talking about. So, what is this thing we all call happiness?

What Is Happiness?

What are we really after when we go on a pursuit of happiness? Though happiness might take different shapes and forms for different people, the basic experience of it remains largely the same. In trying to describe this experience, we could say that happiness is a wholesome state of being, one in which we are fully engaged, self-expressed, and fulfilled. The experience can often be fleeting, such as when we try to attain it through external objects. Conversely, the longest-lasting form of happiness is almost always anchored in a sense of meaning, purpose, or broader awareness. In this way, the essence remains the same, but the depth and breadth of it can shift.

Sometimes, we mistake happiness for a thing we can achieve as if it were as fixed and tangible as a bright and shiny object. However, happiness is not a fixed state of being; it is an inner experience that exists on a continuum. We cannot hold it in our hands, and begging it not to leave us never works. We come into and out of it, but as our personal evolution continues, it becomes easier to tune into some sense of well-being or wholeness, even amidst the storms of life.

The experience of happiness takes place on a spectrum. It comes in different 'flavors' or 'depths' as a whole range of experiences can trigger the rise of this feeling. The spectrum is as follows:

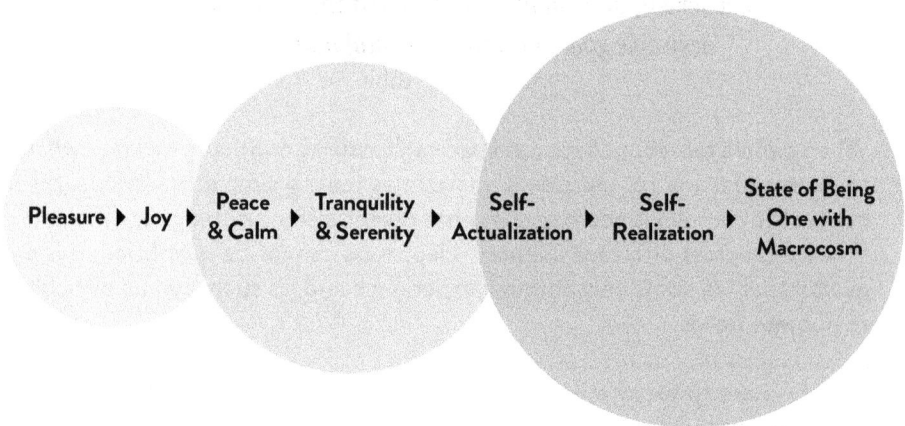

Pleasure ▸ Joy ▸ Peace & Calm ▸ Tranquility & Serenity ▸ Self-Actualization ▸ Self-Realization ▸ State of Being One with Macrocosm

At the beginning of the spectrum, we have feelings like pleasure and joy. These arise when something we perceive to be good or desirable happens. For example, we might feel pleasure when we are blessed to consume a slice of home-baked apple pie. We might feel joy sitting around an evening campfire with good friends.

These examples do not suggest that sitting around the campfire or enjoying a good meal can only bring happiness in the form of pleasure and joy. In fact, we can also tap into other flavors of happiness during these sorts of experiences when qualities such as gratitude, awe, or wonder filter into the experience as well. As explored in the previous chapter, context matters as much as content.

As we commit to self-exploration and personal practice (i.e. through meditation, yoga, prayer, reflection), we are able to experience greater levels of the happiness spectrum. First, we begin to discover the capacity to find peace inside ourselves. Then, we start to realize our unique place and purpose in the world. Finally, after much practice and inquiry, our sense of separation begins to dissolve and we realize our innate connection with all that is: with the macrocosm of life.

This spectrum is not set in stone and different cultures and traditions may interpret it differently. However, understanding the varying flavors of happiness can provide a framework for better understanding our personal evolution into greater depths of fulfillment and purpose.

Happiness Across Time

As touched on above, our human understanding of happiness has evolved across time. We modern human beings are not the first of our kind to ask what it takes to live a good life. Various cultural and historical contexts shape the way we view happiness, the way we pursue it, and the way that we talk about it. We can approach all philosophies of happiness with curiosity and openness, finding value and nuggets of wisdom in a variety of perspectives.

The following exploration of happiness across time and culture is not exhaustive. In fact, the *Atlas of World Cultures* by David H. Price notes over 3814 distinct cultures that have been described by anthropologists.[1] Throughout the course of time, there will certainly have been more human cultures than even what this finger points to. However, it is mentioned to provide a sense of perspective. For every human culture that has existed, there may be additional nuance in the way that happiness is understood.

Vedic Philosophy

To begin this exploration of happiness across time, we can turn towards what we know about happiness as put forth in Vedic philosophy. From the Vedic literature of the Upanishads, we see that the source of truth and joy comes from the eternal.[2] In other words, happiness is a product of being freed of ignorance and of realizing truth. From the Vedantic viewpoint, happiness is our true nature. The recognition of this is *moksha*.[3]

---

1   https://www.ncbi.nlm.nih.gov/pmc/articles/PMC3049104/
2   https://www.dailypioneer.com/2019/columnists/happiness--a-vedantic-view.html
3   https://yogainternational.com/article/view/what-is-happiness

With this perspective, we realize that happiness does not come from outside of ourselves. An object cannot bring happiness as a single object does not provide continued happiness. We can take a pause to reflect here. Have you ever owned or achieved anything that always and continues to bring you happiness? When we sit with this question, we come to realize that no person, object, or place can give us the lasting happiness we desire. In fact, there are many things that in one moment give us a sense of joy or pleasure and in another bring us pain and sadness.

When we obtain an item or live an experience that gives the experience of pleasure, Vedic philosophy tells us that this is *ananda*, pure happiness, that arises as the mind relaxes and we experience our true nature. Ananda, pure happiness or eternal bliss, is the true nature of *Atman*, which is the changeless Self.[4]

Buddhism

Turning toward Buddhism, we see that the conversation is less about happiness and more about liberation from suffering. Liberation begins when we take a look at the Four Noble Truths.[5] They are as follows:

1. Suffering (*dukkha*) – the realization that life involves suffering

2. The causes of suffering – craving and ignorance

3. The end of suffering – realization that what obscures us from truth is temporary and that we can end suffering by ending its causes

4. The path – through ethical conduct, meditation practice, and the cultivation of wisdom, we can journey to the end of suffering

The journey begins with awareness of suffering and then continues as we look into the causes of our suffering. The end of suffering happens when we are able to shift our response to life and thereby cease habits of craving, aversion, and ignorance. And ultimately, we arrive at the path – the Noble Eightfold Path of Buddhism – which entails eight practices:

---

4   https://www.sivanandaonline.org//?cmd=displaysection&section_id=749
5   https://www.lionsroar.com/what-are-the-four-noble-truths/

1. Right understanding

2. Right thought

3. Right speech

4. Right action

5. Right livelihood

6. Right effort

7. Right mindfulness

8. Right Meditation

The eight practices of the path are not steps to be taken one after the next. Rather, they are practiced simultaneously and incorporated into all areas of one's life. So in the Buddhist tradition, happiness is reached when we have purified the mind of mental constructs that obscure our understanding of reality, which is supported by the eightfold path. You would notice that this is remarkably different from the transcendental pursuit of Vedic teachings, making it more 'pragmatic' for an everyday householder life – hence the clearly global appeal of Buddhism.

Christianity

When we look to Christianity for more insight on how the concept of happiness has evolved over time, we discover the belief that ultimate happiness comes through union with God.[6] In fact, some Christians believe that this is the sole source of happiness while others embrace earthly pleasures that come with human life.

In the New Testament, the word *makarios* occurs no less than 50 times. This Greek word, translated as 'blessed', is used largely in the New Testament to express the deep contentment that arises from the fulfillment of salvation. Another word, *chara*, which means 'joy', is seen over 50 times in the New

---

6   https://www.jstor.org/stable/24739086

Testament as well. It is said that this refers to the joy experienced from the realization of *future* salvation.[7]

What we can see here is similar to other ancient religions in that ultimate happiness is understood to be unification with the source of existence. In some religions, that unification is with God (as with Christianity) while in others, it is defined differently. Ultimately, it is about unification with the macrocosm, the universe, or with a higher power.

Islam

In the Holy Qur'an, happiness is understood as something to be experienced both in this world (dunyawiyah) and in the hereafter (ukhrawiyah). The joys of this world are a means to eternal happiness in the next.[8] At the same time, it should be noted that even worldly happiness is distinguished from pure enjoyment, which comes through the physical senses.

Similarly to the identification of causes of suffering in Buddhism, it is important in Islam to identify *shāqawah*, which translates as 'distress', 'misery', 'despair', 'suffering', and so forth. Emotions such as grief, sorrow, narrowness, and fear of the unknown are derived from this suffering.

The term *sa'ādah* is used to express the ultimate form of happiness, which is the highest vision of God and everlasting contentment. Those who act in service of God during this lifetime are granted this infinite happiness: in this lifetime and the hereafter.[9]

Ancient Greece

To speak of the Ancient Greek philosophy of happiness runs the risk of oversimplification as there were many Greek philosophers who each had a unique take on what was required in order to be truly happy. For example, Aristotle described *eudaimonia* (commonly translated as 'happiness' or 'flourishing') to be the highest human good and the only end desirable for

---

7   https://www.publicchristianity.org/some-remarks-on-the-nature-of-happiness/
8   https://yaqeeninstitute.org/read/paper/the-idea-of-happiness-in-the-quran
9   https://www.researchgate.net/publication/335987311_The_Meaning_And_Experience_Of_Happiness_In_Islam_An_Overview

its own sake. In the *Eudemian Ethics*, it was referred to as activity of the soul in accordance with "perfect" or "complete" virtue.[10]

The Stoics of Ancient Greece also believed that virtue was important for happiness. In fact, they believed it was the only thing needed to achieve happiness. Stoics saw passions to be antithetical to a virtuous life and that, rather, one must act to fulfill all personal, professional, and societal responsibilities.[11]

Another Greek philosopher, Epicurus, believed that the only thing to have intrinsic value is one's own pleasure.[12] The rest was seen as valuable only in that it helped to secure future pleasure. At the same time however, Epicurus believed that moderation (along with embodying other virtues) was also needed in the pursuit of happiness.

Importantly, there was also Socrates, who emphasized that the key to being happy is to turn your attention away from the body and towards the soul.[13] He, like many other Greek philosophers, believed in the necessity of virtue in experiencing happiness, and in addition, he believed that self-knowledge and philosophical inquiry could help humans act with greater virtue.[14]

> *"Happiness is the meaning and the purpose of life,*
> *the whole aim and end of human existence."*
> Aristotle

Modern Psychology

As we arrive at the present day, we land in the realms of existential psychology and positive psychology. The first – existential psychology – has its roots in philosophy, with thinkers like Kierkegaard and Nietzsche. It supports humans in coming to terms with the basic truths of human existence. Anxiety, alienation, and meaninglessness are, for instance, seen as inevitable consequences of being alive.[15]

---

10   https://www.britannica.com/topic/eudaimonia
11   https://iep.utm.edu/stoiceth/
12   https://iep.utm.edu/epicur/
13   https://www.pursuit-of-happiness.org/history-of-happiness/socrates/
14   https://academyofideas.com/2013/04/the-ideas-of-socrates/
15   https://www.researchgate.net/publication/228014843_Existential_Psychology

Whereas existential psychology focuses on coming to terms with and alleviating the challenges of being human, positive psychology focuses on how to help humans lead happy, rich, and prosperous lives. It is the study of what makes life worth living. Within this field, obtaining and maintaining happiness is paramount.

Rather than simply aiming for the minimum acceptable degree of well-being, positive psychology aims higher. Shifting from a problem-centric lens, it helps to cultivate positive emotions and experiences, such as optimism, resilience, gratitude, and success.

In 1954, humanistic psychologist Abraham Maslow wrote in his textbook, *Motivation and Personality*:

> *"The science of psychology has been far more successful on the negative than on the positive side; it has revealed to us much about man's shortcomings, his illnesses, his sins, but little about his potentialities, his virtues, his achievable aspirations, or his full psychological height. It is as if psychology had voluntarily restricted itself to only half its rightful jurisdiction, and that the darker, meaner half."* [16]

Since Maslow's time (and even still today in some circles), much of psychology continues to focus on pathology reduction. However, in 1998 when Dr. Martin Seligman was President of the American Psychological Association, one of his core initiatives was the promotion of the scientific study of positive psychology. [17] Since then, positive psychology continues to grow, helping to shed light on the other half of human well-being: the goodness we all wish to experience more of. There are also numerous other contemporary works of researchers like Tal Ben Sharar, Paul Wong, and others who have made significant progress in getting the mainstream, especially the corporate world, to take an interest in happiness in the context of workplace well-being.

---

16   https://reference.jrank.org/people/Abraham_Maslow_19081970.html
17   https://ppc.sas.upenn.edu/people/martin-ep-seligman

Happiness Across Cultures

In addition to traversing the landscape of happiness from past to present, we can take a closer look at happiness as it is understood across cultures today. We cannot assume that modern psychology's understanding of happiness applies to all people throughout the world. Additionally, we can consider that there are many different views and experiences even amongst those who live where modern psychology is most prevalent.

Some of the research that's been conducted looking into differences in perception and experience of happiness across cultures highlights the following:

- People in Western countries associate happiness with exclusively positive emotions whereas East Asian countries often associate it with a mixture of positive and negative emotions.[18]

- North American countries identify happiness more often with high arousal positive affect (i.e. excitement, euphoria) while collectivist Eastern Asians associate happiness with low arousal positive affect (i.e. serenity, tranquility).

- Scandinavians are frequently ranked as the happiest people in the world, but researchers suggest this is not because of a "happy disposition". Rather, it is because of a welfare state that creates the conditions for happiness.[19]

- Dictionary definitions of happiness in the majority of countries – except for Hungary, Italy, Mexico, and North India – include the terms "luck" or "fortune". In the American dictionary, this definition is labeled as "obsolete".

- One study found that in addition to many commonalities in how happiness is defined amongst those in the United States and Japan, key differences existed. For Americans, happiness is more related to a sense of control and high-arousal states whereas, for the Japanese, happiness is related to the fulfillment of other's expectations and low-arousal states.[20]

---

18   https://www.frontiersin.org/articles/10.3389/fpsyg.2016.00030/full#h1
19   https://www.jstor.org/stable/10.5406/scanstud.89.4.0429
20   https://oxford.universitypressscholarship.com/view/10.1093/acprof:o-so/9780199592746.001.0001/acprof-9780199592746-chapter-36

- Another interesting study looked at how the pursuit of happiness predicted well-being across cultures. Motivation to pursue happiness predicted lower well-being in the United States, did not predict well-being in Germany, and in Russia and East Asia, motivation to pursue happiness predicted higher well-being.[21]

- Happiness has been found to be systematically higher in nations that offer a decent material standard of living, freedom, equality, solidarity, and justice.[22]

There are two additional points to make here. The first is that, despite our differences, there are commonalities in what we require for happiness (as the last finding reveals) and in how we define happiness. For example, one study found that many people from all over the world define happiness as a sense of "inner harmony".xviii Perhaps this provides a clue as to what we are really longing for when we go on a search for greater happiness and well-being.

Secondly, it is important to note that there are vast differences among people within a single country or culture. One person might experience or define happiness in a very different way than their neighbor, who is a part of the same community. Without a doubt, you could find individuals who identify with any of the countries, cultures, or religions listed above that would say, "That's not how I see it." Differences in personal philosophy, childhood upbringing, and economic status are just some of the reasons we might not resonate with the dominant perspective of our culture.

Where to Next?

Again, this peek into how happiness has evolved over time and how it presents itself across cultures is by no means complete or absolute. Happiness is continuing to evolve and even in the happiest countries, you will find people with a great deal of suffering. Each human is a complex being, whose view of happiness is as unique as they and their life experience are.

---

21   https://www.ncbi.nlm.nih.gov/pmc/articles/PMC4658246/
22   https://www.internationaljournalofwellbeing.org/index.php/ijow/article/view/98

The following diagram provides an overview of some of the different perspectives on happiness. Some of these we have explored in this chapter and others we will delve into in subsequent chapters. Note that this diagram does not represent a standardized pathway that one must follow in order to experience true happiness. It is simply a snapshot of the predominant viewpoints and hypotheses of our time.

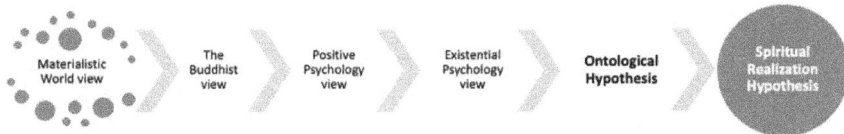

I would love to wax eloquent about the figure above, there is clearly a whole other book here and of course a subject matter close to my heart. But I will summarize by saying that the lens you choose to look at happiness with defines the lived experience you will find. It is helpful to think of it as the spectrum of a rainbow, where each color is unique, and yet there are two ends we can approach it from!

So where do we go from here? After all these centuries, have we gotten any closer to discovering where true happiness resides? Unfortunately, this does not appear to be the case. If happiness was as easy as steps 1-2-3, we would not be facing the mental health crisis that is with us now.

For starters, we might consider shifting our focus from achieving "happiness" to reaching "wholesomeness". The shift is subtle, but the term "wholesomeness" includes meaning, purpose, engagement, and the capacity to nurture and share positive emotions. To be "whole" welcomes all of our human experience, whereas happiness may feel too idealistic or narrowly focused for many modern humans.

The shift to wholesomeness also invites us to consider: *What are the virtues or qualities that contribute to a holistic sense of well-being?* Rather than focusing on the feeling of happiness as the "be-all-end-all", we might consider that well-being is something that arises when a set of virtues are nurtured (i.e. gratitude, goodwill, inner peace, calm, patience, generosity, and so on).

Additionally, we need to consider that, while there is much wisdom and value in ancient understandings, we are living in a completely different world than any of our ancestors. Modern-day living has increased the complexity and challenges of reaching a state of wholesomeness, so we must take these new conditions into consideration.

Perhaps finding our way to happiness – or wholesomeness – requires an approach that is both new and old: one that draws on ancient wisdom and also honors the challenges of the present day, enabling us to effectively navigate the conditions we live in now. Let's move forward by taking a look at some of the unique, modern life challenges that impact all of us before we dive further into how we might overcome them.

Journal Exercise: Pause for Reflection

Take a moment to find a quiet place to sit with a journal and a pen. Holding in heart and mind what we explored in this chapter, read through the following questions and write down your responses. There are no 'right' or 'wrong' answers. Simply use this as an opportunity for deeper inquiry.

1. What similarities did you observe in the viewpoints of happiness explored in this chapter? What differences did you observe?

2. What perspectives resonate most with you? What were certain perspectives lacking from your viewpoint?

3. How does it feel to shift from the word 'happiness' to 'wholesomeness' or 'well-being'?

4. At this moment, how would you define happiness, wholesomeness, or well-being? Choose the term that resonates the most with you and try to encapsulate in words what it means to you.

A Buddhist, a Researcher and a Mom

One of the things I learned early on in my career from a very unlikely source, that of a foreign affairs analyst, was *"focus not on what people say, rather on what people do"*. In pursuit of my own lived research on the subject of happiness, I went to the usual suspects, starting with some Buddhist scholars – especially since in the secular context much interest has been generated in the wisdom of Buddhist teachings. During this exploration, I attended many retreats, one of which stands out to me.

I was in a silent retreat with about a dozen other participants, and we had a senior resident monk assigned to us to mentor our progress with meditation. The monk would also give a daily *dhamma talk*. One frequent subject that came up was that of happiness and how attachment to material things was a root cause of much of the *'suffering'* or more generally a lack of satisfaction. One day, the mentoring monk delivered a wonderful dhamma talk on *Dvayatanupassana Sutta*, and we had an interesting discussion on the need for approaching things with empathy, as a foundation for lasting happiness. The next day was a Tuesday, and we were expecting a visiting monk to come and lecture to us. Suddenly in the afternoon, one of the fellow retreat attendees (a mom) got a message from her family that her young child was not doing well and would likely be hospitalized. She was understandably worried and went to the Abbot to seek his permission to leave.

The retreat center was somewhat off the major traffic route so no public transport was available, and the mentoring monk was deputed to drive the participant to the nearest bus station. He didn't look pleased, which was a bit surprising to note. I volunteered to accompany them and off we went in the car driving about ninety minutes to the nearest town. The monk was mostly silent for the majority of the trip and I busied myself with emotionally supporting the participant. He did speak up a little bit, indirectly chiding the participant about leaving the retreat midway, even though her husband and family were there to fully take care of the child. He made the point to her that she was not a doctor and, to that extent, she was operating from 'fear' rather than from 'detachment'. While philosophically sound, it seemed like a harsh thing to say in the moment. Anyway, she was soon on a bus back to the city and we were free to return to the retreat center.

On the way back, I asked the monk if he wanted to stop to eat something as it was getting late and I knew he wouldn't be able to eat any food when the sun went down. While we were sitting at a roadside eatery, I asked him why he was so quiet. He replied a little churlishly that he didn't understand why the Abbot sent him on this trip, knowing fully well that he would miss the dhamma talk from the visiting monk. There were so many others he could have sent, why a senior monk like him? He seemed very contrite, if not upset.

I was stunned. Not only did I not expect this outburst from the monk, but I had a really hard time rationalizing the wise, eloquent exponent of empathy and acceptance I had witnessed the day before with this version of an upset and complaining person in front of me.

I guess that was early in my years and I was very naïve. Since then, I have gone on to meet researchers on mindfulness that don't have any practice (but published credits), leadership gurus that can not build a team around themselves, doctors that are very unhealthy, and conferences on workplace happiness where people argue whose model is better. So I guess my conclusion from this was: knowing what happiness is even at a deep philosophical level does not equal to 'being happy' or living it!

This point was further clarified when the participant texted me a picture of her holding her baby and literally glowing with joy and love. So sure, she may not have internalized the Buddhist path of happiness but had found a moment of access to it to savor!

CHAPTER 4

The Hedonic Treadmill of Modern Life

How can it be that with all the modern advances that have been granted to us over the years, we are no closer to happiness than our ancestors? One might assume or imagine that happiness *must* be on the rise as medicine develops, technology makes many facets of daily life easier, and access to things like travel and leisure increases.

Yet despite these measurable improvements in the way that many of us live our lives, modern life has also brought with it a number of challenges, which we will explore in this chapter and the next. One of these challenges is the paradox of choice and the hedonic treadmill we have unwittingly found ourselves on.

The Paradox of Choice & the Consumerist Trap

We have more 'things' to make us happy than any of our ancestors could have dreamed of. New gadgets, state-of-the-art home appliances, and social media technologies are just a few of the modern advancements that claim to make our lives easier and more pleasurable. And yet, some figures suggest that rather than being on the rise, happiness is on the decline in many places. The General Social Survey conducted in the United States shows that general happiness amongst adults has been slowly declining since around the year 2000.[23]

Barry Schwartz, author of the book The Paradox of Choice, explores one reason that we are no happier than we were before, and that is this abundance of choice itself. Rather than freeing us, Schwartz proposes that all of this

---

23	https://worldhappiness.report/ed/2019/the-sad-state-of-happiness-in-the-united-states-and-the-role-of-digital-media/

choice leaves us feeling paralyzed and dissatisfied rather than fulfilled.[24] In his 2005 TED Talk, Schwartz notes:[25]

> *"All of this choice has two effects, two negative effects on people. One effect, paradoxically, is that it produces paralysis rather than liberation. With so many options to choose from, people find it very difficult to choose at all."*

He continues to highlight the second negative impact:

> *"The second effect is that even if we manage to overcome the paralysis and make a choice, we end up less satisfied with the result of the choice than we would be if we had fewer options to choose from."*

As Schwartz explains, this abundance of choice can lead us to feeling regret if we later feel like we made the wrong choice. In addition, it becomes easy to imagine the positive aspects of all the things we said 'no' to, which makes the choice we *did* make feel less satisfying.

What do we do when we feel unsatisfied? Ultimately, we have two choices: to look deeper into the root causes of our dissatisfaction or to look beyond ourselves. The first is challenging but necessary, and yet modern society does not support us in taking that closer look. With marketing for consumer products just a click away, it is easy to become pulled into another purchase.

When we look beyond ourselves for a solution, thinking that satisfaction is somewhere 'out there', we are likely to get caught in the consumerist trap. Whether consciously or unconsciously, the consumerist trap is driven by the belief that the *next* thing (i.e. the new car, further house renovations, the new shoes) will bring us the fulfillment that we crave.

There is neuroscience to explain how this works in the brain. One research study found that just asking people to look at products they deemed to be 'cool' activated a part of the brain called the medial prefrontal cortex. The

---

24   https://www.npr.org/2012/05/04/151879693/does-having-options-make-us-happier?t=1631606832351
25   https://www.ted.com/talks/barry_schwartz_the_paradox_of_choice

activation pattern was similar to what happens in the brain when we receive a compliment or feel valued.[26]

Additionally, when we are scrolling online retail outlets or preparing to make a purchase elsewhere, the anticipation alone of receiving some reward or desirable item increases dopamine secretion.[27] Dopamine is the neurotransmitter often referred to as the 'feel-good hormone'.

Yet, as most of us know through experience, lasting happiness is never found in a single item. In many cases, it brings us a sense of joy or pleasure for a short while, but sooner rather than later, the contentment with the item fades and we end up back where we started, yearning for something more.

The Treadmill of Hedonic Adaptation

'Hedonic adaptation' is a concept that describes why the pleasure doesn't last. It refers to the notion that after a positive or negative event and an increase in positive or negative feelings as a result, we return to a baseline level of effect or happiness. Why does this happen? According to the insight of hedonic adaptation, it is because our *perception* of how positive or negative something is changed. In fact, our perception of the item, reward, or achievement neutralizes as we adapt to our new reality.[28]

This scientific perspective adds weight to ancient spiritual traditions that see happiness not as something that comes from certain objects but rather from within. No single object, relationship, or experience can offer us the happiness we desire because happiness is not inherent to it.

When left unrecognized and unexamined, this rise and fall in surface-level happiness (or enjoyment) can lead us to a continual pursuit of pleasure. We crave the positive feelings we experienced when we attained that new job, new relationship, or flashy new item (even if only temporary), and so we yearn for the next one. This is the hedonic treadmill – the constant pursuit of the next best thing to bring us another spark of enjoyment, contentment, or pleasure.

---

26   https://www.pbs.org/newshour/economy/consumerism-make-us-happy-surprising-answers-looking-inside-consumers-brain
27   https://health.clevelandclinic.org/retail-therapy-shopping-compulsion/
28   https://www.sciencedirect.com/topics/psychology/hedonic-adaptation

Hedonic Treadmill

Desire

Strive

Adapt

Enjoy

Obtain/
Buy

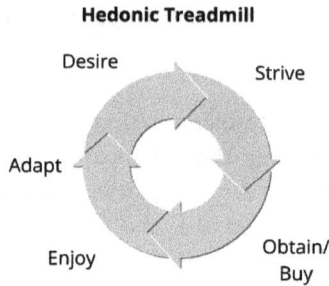

Hedonic adaptation also works, as alluded to in the original definition, when negative events occur. For example, if we make a big mistake at work or in front of friends, we may feel temporarily overcome by feelings of embarrassment, but the feelings do not last. In the same way, we recover from grief and sorrow after experiencing loss, returning to our baseline level of effect or happiness over time.

We often forget the truth that even in the face of negative experiences, we hold immense power to 'bounce back.' This ability to recover from emotional or psychological difficulties is what Daniel Gilbert, Ph.D. and Timothy Wilson, Ph.D. refer to as "psychological immune system". They note that, through research, it appears that many of us forget that we have such a capacity. They also found that people typically overestimate the duration of unhappiness following negative events.[29]

What does this have to do with satisfaction and happiness? Gilbert notes that one of the reasons we underestimate how quickly our feelings can change is that we don't fully recognize our power to change them. He adds: "This can lead us to make decisions that don't maximize our potential for satisfaction".

Another concept put forth by Gilbert and Wilson is that of 'miswanting'. Miswanting refers to the fact that people often mistake how much they will enjoy something in the future.[30] For example, we might think that moving into a larger apartment will make us happier because of x, y, and z reasons, but when we move in, we find that our expectations for happiness are left unreached.

---

29   https://www.apa.org/monitor/oct01/strength
30   https://www.apa.org/science/about/psa/2004/04/pelham

This could be due to overly focusing on one aspect of our experience as the cause of our current dissatisfaction, but perhaps it is also related to our misunderstanding about what truly brings happiness. If we were raised in a modern society (as most of us reading this book were), we were surrounded by messages that reaffirmed the allure of consumerism. In other words, if we have come to believe that attaining the perfect look or a reputable job or a cool car is a primary cause of happiness, we come by this belief naturally. Our modern cultural context created the conditions for this belief to take root.

As we begin to bear witness to this cycle of desiring, striving, and attaining, and as we tune into our baseline level of contentment, we might start to reassess our habits, cravings, and goals. This process of reassessment holds immense power, helping to clear the fog of illusion and help us discover a way of being in the world that brings us true well-being and fulfillment.

> *"We don't have to wait for the right circumstances*
> *to have happiness."*
> Rupert Spira

Seeing Through the Illusion

To break through the illusion that consumption can bring us happiness, we must first recognize that we are in fact on a treadmill. We need to become more curious about what beliefs we hold about where happiness comes from and how we can obtain it. We cannot change anything that we are not aware of.

We also need to recognize that our perceptions and expectations don't always match up with reality. For instance, it is okay if we think that renovating another corner of the house will bring us contentment and that that will be enough, but can we recognize that this is simply an expectation? We do not need to make the expectation 'right' or 'wrong', but it is helpful to realize that our assumptions are not fact. Can we get more curious about our desires, hopes, and expectations?

Additionally, it is helpful to consider that what we expect will bring us happiness is always relative – to where we are in life, to what messages we are sold, and to what other people are doing around us. Media, marketing, and social comparison play considerable roles in what we think we need, oftentimes leading us to 'miswant' things that will not, in the end, improve our state of well-being. For example, the phrase "keeping up with the Joneses" highlights our human tendency to make comparisons, chasing not what we *actually* want but what others want or what we feel we 'should' want.

It is also helpful to be mindful of the cognitive tendency of impact bias. Impact bias is the tendency to overestimate how good or bad something will make us feel, and for how long. For example, think of a time when you desired something very strongly. Perhaps it was a job, a new item of clothing, a piece of furniture, or a romantic relationship. Often, when we have such strong desires for something, there is also the thought that "When I obtain this, I will finally be happy. *This* will be enough." Have you ever wanted something so much that you believed it would be enough?

The truth is that if happiness comes from something outside of us, it will never be enough. We will adapt to our new circumstances and soon find ourselves craving something else. As a result, so long as we are seeking happiness from some external object, relationship, or recognition, we will be on a continual search.

Keep in mind that the impact bias also occurs when we anticipate the impact of a negative experience. For example, if we fear speaking our truth because we will lose a job or a friend, we might overestimate the intensity and/or duration of the difficulty this action would cause. Thanks to our psychological immune system, we typically recover far quicker than we believe we will.

We can also begin to conceptually see through the illusions of consumption by realizing that in the majority of cases, more money does not mean more happiness. In fact, it has largely been stated that income only increases subjective well-being when people are trying to get their basic needs met.[31] Laurie Santos, Ph.D., touches on this during a talk she gave at the Aspen Ideas Festival, noting that often, as our income increases, so too does our yearning for something greater.[32] This she refers to as a forecasting error. This error occurs when what we think will make us happier turns out to be inaccurate.

---

31   https://www.jstor.org/stable/27526987
32   https://www.youtube.com/watch?v=ZizdBOTgAVM

In order for these statements and findings to truly help you see through the illusion, you need to feel into them for yourself. In other words, someone telling you that shiny objects will not provide you with lasting happiness is something you can only believe when you assess the statement in relation to your own experience.

To deepen your sense of what has been suggested here, consider the following reflection questions. Write your answers down in a journal.

- Call to mind something that you once accomplished or obtained that brought you an experience of joy or contentment. This could be a material object, a job, or a relationship. Once you have it in mind, consider:

  » Did the happiness of receiving/obtaining this job, object, or relationship last permanently? If it is still present with you and sometimes offers a sense of joy, does it *always* make you happy? If the joy it sparks fades or changes, is it accurate to say that *it* is the cause of your happiness?

- Are there things in your life you have worked towards that you thought you *should* obtain or experience? In other words, are there things you have strived towards or purchased that, upon deeper reflection, were not in alignment with your deepest wishes?

- What beliefs do you hold about happiness? Write them all down, knowing that some of the beliefs you hold may be contradictory with other ones. Reflect further by asking each belief if it is *absolutely* true.

Working With Our Baseline

Once we begin to see through the illusion of the consumerist trap and wish to step off the hedonic treadmill, we might still be left wondering:

Where do I go from here?

Stepping off the hedonic treadmill does not ensure immediate happiness because we are left simply with our baseline level of contentment and, typically, if we are caught up in the race of consumption, our baseline is not where it could be.

This is one of the reasons many people fear looking too closely at this cyclical pattern of consumerism. To look at it requires us to acknowledge that we may not be as happy as we wish to be. It requires courage, patience, and compassion to lean in and examine this, so if you are here doing this work, congratulations. You have an inner strength that will see you through this journey of ever-expanding awareness.

The question then is:

How do I increase my baseline happiness?

The good news is that, as mentioned in the previous chapter, modern psychology is taking a closer look at not just how to reduce pathology but also how to *increase* positive experiences. Increasing positive experiences in this sense is not about getting quick fixes as we do through consumption; it is about shifting our overall state of being to one of greater well-being.

In his work in the field of positive psychology, Dr. Martin Seligman has conducted research to explore positive interventions that could lead to higher degrees of happiness long term. For example, one study assessed five happiness interventions, two of which resulted in greater happiness and less depression up to six months later. A third produced considerable positive changes for one month.[33]

The simple interventions that resulted in the longest positive impact were:

- Writing about three good things that happened each day for one week and commenting on why they happened

- Using signature strengths of character in a new way each day for one week (after identifying their top five strengths from an inventory of character strengths)

The intervention that showed a positive impact for one month was:

- Writing and delivering a letter of gratitude to a person who had been especially kind to them but never properly thanked

---

33   https://www.researchgate.net/publication/7701091_Positive_Psychology_Progress_Empirical_Validation_of_Interventions

While six months is not indicative of 'happiness for a lifetime', it suggests that there are indeed ways of increasing our basic sense of well-being beyond simply receiving a short boost of positive emotion. For instance, consider the impact of making a new, highly desired purchase. How long, if you were to guess, does this new purchase typically increase your baseline happiness? It is worth mindfully sitting with this question and exploring what happens when we practice these other methods put forth by Seligman and his team.

Now, one might argue that their baseline level of happiness feels set in stone. After all, many of us have struggled with the same general state of well-being for much of our lives. Sonja Lyubomirsky, Ph.D., addresses the finding that approximately 50% of our happiness lies in genetics.[34] While this might seem to be quite high, what is the potential that rests in the other 50%?

She notes that another 10% of our capacity for happiness (give or take) comes from our life circumstances and another 40% (approximately) comes from intentional activity. This is where we have room to grow – and 40% is a pretty large room.

Once these figures were established, the next question was: What do happy people have in common? In one of her presentations, she notes that happy people tend to feel more comfortable expressing gratitude, help others, practice optimism about the future, savor pleasures of the present moment, prioritize physical activity, are frequently spiritual or religious, and are committed to lifelong goals.

These findings do not necessarily indicate that performing these actions cause happiness; rather, they are correlated with happiness. Regardless, they do offer us insight into some of the actions and behaviors that are common to those who experience greater happiness. Through application and personal exploration, we can discover for ourselves whether implementing any number of the above-mentioned tendencies sparks an increase in our well-being.

What else can we consider to increase our baseline level of happiness? Dr. Seligman's PERMA™ theory of well-being outlines five building blocks that enable human flourishing: Positive Emotions, Engagement, Relationships, Meaning, and Accomplishment.[35] Each can be enhanced through practice.

34   https://www.youtube.com/watch?v=_URP3-V1sY4
35   https://ppc.sas.upenn.edu/learn-more/perma-theory-well-being-and-perma-workshops

The building blocks are as follows:

Positive Emotion – Positive emotions, a hedonic pursuit, can be increased in relation to the past, the present, and the future. Techniques for enhancing positive emotions include cultivating forgiveness, savoring current blessings, and building optimism.

Engagement – Engagement occurs when an individual fully utilizes their skills, strength, and capacity for attention during a difficult task. This creates a sense of "flow" and it can be cultivated during any number of activities (i.e. conversing with a friend or stranger, creating art, building a house or furniture, etc.).

Relationships – Well-being is increased through relational experiences and through the joy, meaning, laughter, and belonging that can arise when we feel connected. By cultivating strong relationships, we strengthen this building block.

Meaning – Being of service to something bigger than oneself is another building block of human flourishing, which can come from finding meaning in things such as spirituality, social causes, family, or science.

Accomplishment – Lastly, working to accomplish something, whether that be at work, at home, in art, or elsewhere, provides a sense of fulfillment, even when it does not lead to positive emotions or greater meaning. Setting goals and working towards them can help to strengthen this building block.

As we consider ways of increasing our baseline level of happiness, we must first recognize that doing so is possible. While each of us has come into this world with certain predispositions that shape the way we move through life, there is considerable potential to shift our experience. By recognizing that greater happiness is possible, we create space to begin crafting the life that will fulfill us on a deeper level.

Once we find that space and potential within ourselves, we can start to powerfully assess the areas in which we have room to grow. For example, we might ask ourselves:

- Can I begin to express more gratitude?

- Can I start to savor more present-moment beauty?

- Can I work on cultivating greater forgiveness, compassion, optimism, hope, and other values and virtues?

- Can I engage more fully in the world, sharing more of my unique strengths and skills?

- Do I need to begin by identifying my unique gifts and strengths?

- Where can I find more meaning in my life and in the work that I do, whether professionally or outside of work?

- Is there room to set clear goals that are in alignment with what truly matters to me?

- Can I shift the way that I show up for the difficulties in my life?

- Can I recognize any misunderstandings I may hold about where happiness comes from?

- Am I willing to cultivate new habits of happiness?

This list of questions is not exhaustive of the inquiry we can begin, but it can serve as a starting point, increasing self-awareness and planting seeds of potential. However, there are further conditions of the modern world that need to be considered when stepping forward into a more fulfilling way of being. It is these additional concerns that play a role in why it is so difficult for some to reconnect with the actions and virtues associated with happiness – and that is the digital disruption of our times.

A Sense of Connection

In the journey of deepening our appreciation of the esoteric phenomenon of happiness, there is a dimension that for now lies largely underappreciated by modern psychology - *happiness as a sense of connection or rigorously seeking connectedness.*

Going beyond engagement, meaning, and purpose, there lies a subtle yet profoundly liberating feeling of being one with a larger whole. For some, the larger whole relates to the collective humanity while, to others, it means mother nature and even the macrocosm or the cosmos. This conversation may seem to belong mostly in the realm of new-age spirituality and yet, when experienced, this ontology unfolds a deep level of inner harmony that is hard to capture in words, and certainly much more profound than the flavor of happiness suggests. And it can arise regardless of what the circumstance of our physical, material, and other dimensions of life might be when we are ready.

It may seem I have digressed a bit from the empirical tone of the chapter, but I would have felt remiss if I did not close the conversation here without leaving a seed thought. A big part of the conversation about happiness and joy actually entails deepening and enriching our imagination of an ever greater sense of possible wholesomeness A conversation I have tried to have many times with my positive psychology colleagues and philosophy colleagues, often without much success, encouraged me to leave this inquiry in your hands, to unfold as you are intuitively guided to – happy surfing!

Journal Exercise: Pause for Reflection

Before moving on to the next chapter, take some time to reflect on the following questions. These questions are inspired by the above points of inquiry, probing even further to increase our awareness of practical steps we can take in service of our highest potential for well-being. Write down your answers in a journal.

1. What are my unique strengths, gifts, or skills? Remember that you do not need to be perfect at something to excel at it.

2. What clear goals can I set that are in alignment with what truly matters to me?

3. What would it take for me to shift the way that I show up for life's challenges?

4. What can I be grateful for today? How can I express that gratitude?

5. What brings me a sense of meaning and how can I make a greater commitment to that?

If you do not have clear answers to all of the above questions, that is okay. Answer as best as you can and trust that holding the question is enough to create an inner shift. As time passes, deeper insights and clarity will arise.

A Diva, an Altruist, and a Healer

At a rather vulnerable phase of my life, I developed a friendship with a wonderful human being who I will call Dee. I met her at a non-profit event, where she had quietly stood out to me as she volunteered for the most unpleasant of tasks (think cleaning toilets) with a very cheery attitude. As I got to know her better, I realized that she was a person with a deep empathy for challenging circumstances of life and a genuine desire to be of service. She would be found everywhere, helping everyone in every way she could. I know it sounds like a mouthful, but that was her!

We bonded quickly and eventually, I asked her what inspired her, she said it made her *feel happy* – it made sense to me at that time. Later, as our social circles overlapped more, I realized that in all settings she would talk non-stop about her desire to be of service, often even when no one was asking her, and even when the conversation felt forced, as she went on and on about all that needs to be changed in the world. Slowly, I began to realize that her volunteer portfolio was in some ways motivated by her need to feel special within her circle of otherwise 'sophisticated and accomplished' people.

I also noticed that when she arrived at most places, she would be immaculately put together, very fashionable, and brand conscious – clearly with a somewhat of an axiomatic presentation compared to the values of austerity or pretenseless service she would talk about. As we traveled together a bit, I realized she consciously curated which brands to walk in with at which settings, and she slowly started coaching me on why I should pay attention to it as well because this is how people judge other people (*I of course remained a bad student, and even today no one can accuse me of being fashionable ☺*).

However, I found this rather odd and out of line with her stated intent of a 'minimalist life' and 'pleasure of service rather than possessions'. Why then so much of a struggle to want to fit in? When I put this question to her, she responded that she *feels happy* this way.

What was even more surprising to me was that this was all clearly outside of her means of living and she was continuously spending way more than she could afford, struggling with cash flow/expense, while curating an image of 'successful' to fit in with her crowd. Once, when she was in a substantial financial mess, I confronted her as a friend and asked why she didn't moderate her spending, live within her means, and I got the same answer back: she *felt happy* when she spent money.

And then I asked her a question that, in retrospect, I realized affected our relationship: 'Dee, what makes you happier – serving, feeling special, spending money? What feeling lasts longer? She did not respond to my question, just saying, 'This is how I am,' before moving on.

That evening, I realized that unless we pay close attention to our hedonic rewards treadmill, the pursuit of happiness can quickly become about filling an *ever deeper hole* or a race for more and more – never arriving at enough – instead of being a journey of nurturing wholesomeness standing in freedom and joy. I guess, this is where lies the boundaries of *pleasure* or *reward*-based unfoldment of what we may momentarily feel is happiness. And the being of lasting joy and fulfillment that arises from within.

CHAPTER 5

Digitally Disrupted Generations

We often forget that life isn't the same now as it was not that long ago. Our modern societies have changed rapidly and just as adaptation occurs when we're on the hedonic treadmill, so too have we adapted to the new reality created by modernity. How would we function, for instance, if our internet went off for an hour? A day? A week? We have become highly reliant upon the world of digital technology, forgetting that there were other ways humans got things done in the not-so-distant past.

The hedonic treadmill accelerates within the presence of digital technologies. It intensifies how quickly we can receive that next rush of dopamine, validation, or sense of being seen. We rapidly consume content, messages, marketing, and images when they are just a click away, so in order to find fulfillment in this modern age, we must also increase our awareness of how the digital world is impacting our sense of well-being.

Life in a Virtual World

What does it mean to live in a virtual world? Each one of us still lives in the physical reality of our four-walled home and still engages in the tangible community or natural environment surrounding us. Those things have not gone away since digitalization took root, but a new type of online world established itself in tandem with digitalization – the virtual world.

As more and more of life takes place in this virtual reality, we lose touch with the real, felt, human-to-human, human-to-earth experiences of life. Real flowers are being replaced with emojis, online games are detracting from time spent playing outdoors, and breakups, one of life's more challenging interactions, are being delivered through text.

In many ways, digitalization has made things easier for us. We can send notes of 'love' more quickly through our phones and we do not need to fully show up for life's challenges. Breakups, for instance, are painful for both parties, but if done mindfully, they offer us room to recognize our shared humanity, to learn, and grow. What have we lost with the convenience and speed of digitalization?

Additionally, although we still have real homes, real friends, and real environments around us to explore, we now also have virtual homes, virtual friends, and even virtual lives that include families and communities. Many online games, for example, simulate the external characteristics of a community. I would argue, however, that they fail to capture the heart and soul – the internal characteristics – of human life and community.

Social networks, too, simulate our tangible, in-person communities. We maintain (even if only technically speaking) online friendships, we browse online marketplaces, and we gather in clubs and groups online. While there are many benefits of being able to connect with others through online mediums (which we'll touch on further on), these social networks often lack the depth and breadth that our in-person support systems contain. For example, we can have online 'friends' and not know anything about them except for the parts of their life they choose to share in snapshots. Social media fails to capture the nuance, complexity, and multifaceted nature of humanity.

The various aspects of digitalization, no matter which ones we choose to engage in, shift our engagement with the world because they provide easy access to pleasure. As mentioned earlier, just the act of looking for something to buy can increase dopamine levels in the brain. Previously, we needed to get in our car or hop on the train in order to see what the shops had for sale. Now, we can browse the contents of any shop from anywhere – and at any hour of the day.

Similarly, social media usage shifts dopamine production in the brain. Research has shown that rewarding social stimuli, such as positive recognition or smiling faces, activate our brain's dopamine pathways.[36] This type of stimuli is available at our fingertips and all we need to do is make a post that will trigger a notification or a 'like'. As dopamine is released, the feeling reinforces the behavior that triggered it. It encourages us to repeat it, posting again for our next boost of that feel-good hormone.

---

36   https://sitn.hms.harvard.edu/flash/2018/dopamine-smartphones-battle-time/

As we begin to correlate our online behaviors with 'feel good' sensations, we will be less willing to engage in activities that don't give us the spark we are looking for. Could this be why many people find it more difficult to read a book these days? The presence and patience required to get into a new novel are not as rewarding for the brain as another scroll through the social feed.

While some might argue that digital technologies support our cognitive evolution due to the access they grant us to unthinkable amounts of information, this is up for debate. Could it be that, rather than promoting cognitive-social evolution, this new normal is causing our social-cognitive abilities to atrophy? I do not know the answer to this, but the question is worth asking.

Instead of posing these difficult questions, it seems that the modern collective has normalized this new way of engaging with the 'world'. For instance, we talk openly and with great care when the topics of drug, alcohol, and gambling addictions come up. But this virtual world has brought with it new addictions – addictions to social media, television, and the news. Have we fully recognized the risks of this? There is also the concern of compulsive working out or addiction to plastic surgery as a result of the obsession with body image.

While these are all different addictions on the surface, the basic pathology is the same. Research has found that all addictive drugs increase the release of dopamine in the brain – the same chemical that increases when we are searching for our next purchase or when we receive a 'thumbs up' of approval.[37] Every time we engage in the behavior that provides this dopamine boost, we strengthen the neural circuits associated with this action. As a result, an addiction is created.

Furthermore, the virtual world has shifted where we find inspiration from. Rather than finding meaning, beauty, and influence from the world around us, it comes from within the bubble of social media. The Kardashian Effect speaks to the influence that social media has on the human psyche. Many people, girls and young women in particular, now want to live just like the Kardashians. What if they had the same exposure to people like Marie Curie,

---

37   https://dana.org/article/how-addiction-hijacks-our-reward-system/

Mother Teresa, Simone Biles, or Cheryl Sandberg? What would life be like then? What would *their* life be like then?

The above points to what life is like when we are immersed in the virtual world. This new online reality shapes our values, our beliefs, and the allocation of our time and energy. Virtual reality is the online manifestation of the hedonic treadmill. Even though what we are consuming is not tangible, we are still engaging in this cyclical rhythm of craving, seeking, attaining, and then returning to the start. Let's dive deeper into some of the other impacts of technologization.

The Impact of Technologization

What has the pervasiveness of digital media consumption led to? Before we explore some of the other drawbacks, let's touch on some of the benefits. It isn't all bad, is it?

The digital era has led to great advances in medicine, research, science, and distribution (among other realms of life). In terms of daily life, it has also provided us with great benefits: the ability for many of us to work from anywhere, the ability to stay in touch with people no matter the physical distance, the ability to find information quickly and readily, the ability to accomplish daily tasks like banking in less time, and the ability to meet new people or connect with groups we might not have otherwise been able to. These are just some of the benefits that digital technology has granted us.

But as this is a book on happiness and well-being, we need to look at the overall impact of this new virtual world we find ourselves in. How does it impact our state of wellness? Is it ultimately supportive of and conducive to well-being or is it working against happiness?

While the benefits are certainly not to be ignored or brushed aside, we need to ensure that the technology we are engaging with has a net positive impact on our lives. Once we have a sense of the drawbacks of the virtual world, we can work towards a harmonious relationship with technology that maximizes what is beneficial and minimizes that which is detrimental. How can we change our online behavior to make *it* work for *us*?

Loneliness

To get a better sense of what too much technology usage might be leading to, we can take a look at the impact of social media on loneliness, as it has been found that loneliness is negatively correlated with subjective happiness and life satisfaction.[38] In one study of 143 undergraduate students, it was found that limiting social media use to approximately 30 minutes per day led to a significant improvement in well-being. In comparison with a control group, the group that limited Facebook, Instagram, and Snapchat usage showed reductions in loneliness and depression over three weeks.[39]

When we look at a study that focused on older adults, we find that technology largely supported well-being by *reducing* loneliness.[40] This is an important finding and a point for consideration because it acknowledges that across the lifespan, we may be in need of different support systems. Older adults who live alone or who are retired may rely more on digital connections for staying in touch with family and friends.

Breakdown of Families and Communities

Another area of concern is the potential for virtual reality to detract from the well-being of and connection to family and community members. As more time is spent online, we spend less time with those in our immediate environment. In other words, while we put more energy into maintaining online communities, we detract from the energy that we might spend caring for our loved ones and our neighbors.

There is nothing wrong with cultivating an online community. In fact, many people might cultivate very valuable connections with people through online mediums that they would not have been able to make otherwise. However, we must remember that our online connections should not come at the expense of our in-person connections.

---

38   https://www.ncbi.nlm.nih.gov/pmc/articles/PMC4873114/
39   https://guilfordjournals.com/doi/abs/10.1521/jscp.2018.37.10.751
40   https://www.liebertpub.com/doi/10.1089/cyber.2016.0151

Mental Health

Another major cause for concern is the research that found a sudden decline in happiness and life satisfaction among adolescents in the United States after 2012.[41] This came right around the same time that the majority of Americans owned smartphones. Adolescents spent less time engaging in screen-free activities and, in fact, the only activity that adolescents spent more time doing during the last decade is using digital media. Another finding from a similar time period shows that since 2010, depression, suicidal ideation, and self-harm have increased considerably among adolescents, particularly in girls and young women.

From the World Happiness Report, we can also see which activities are correlated with general happiness. Sleep, exercise, and in-person social interaction have the highest correlation to general happiness while listening to music, spending time on the internet, and computer games show the lowest correlation.

Research has also found a connection between social media usage and anxiety. One study focusing on emerging adults (aged 18 to 22 years old) found that more daily social media use was significantly correlated with an increased likelihood of a probable anxiety disorder.[42]

Creativity and Problem-solving

When it comes to creativity and problem-solving, social media can also be detrimental. First, creativity requires that we are imaginative and inventive, and that we take risks. What we manifest through creativity is not always 'cool' or 'popular' so social media can hinder our willingness to take such creative risks. It is easier to share or create something that we know will be liked than to risk thinking or creating outside the box, particularly if we are hooked on the dopamine that comes from social acceptance online.

In terms of problem-solving, research done by Patricia Greenfield, Ph.D., suggests that as technology has become more central to our lives, our capacity for critical thinking and analysis has decreased while our visual skills

---

41   https://worldhappiness.report/ed/2019/the-sad-state-of-happiness-in-the-united-states-and-the-role-of-digital-media/

42   https://www.sciencedirect.com/science/article/abs/pii/S0165032716309442

have improved.[43] Reading, which has declined amongst younger generations as digital media has soared, can help strengthen imagination, reflection, and critical thinking – all key aspects of effective problem-solving.

Life Skills

Another drawback of modernity and its fixation with technology is the lack of basic life skills that younger generations are developing. This comes back to the fact that more time is being spent online than in 'real life'. Rather than going camping, for instance, many youths occupy themselves by playing video games or watching various forms of media. Even though we do not necessarily 'need' outdoor wilderness skills to survive in modern times, we cannot underestimate the important teachings that can be relayed through exploring nature or even just enjoying one's own backyard. In fact, one study found that time spent outdoors and in nature enhanced adolescents' resilience to stressors, including the COVID-19 pandemic.[44]

Social and Relational Skills

When it comes to the impact of technology on social skills, the jury seems to be out. There are conflicting data and opposing conclusions drawn by various researchers. However, there is some evidence to suggest that children who access online gaming or social networking many times a day have reduced social skills as compared to their peers.[45]

We can also think about this from an intuitive perspective, coming back to the idea that many relationships are ending via text. With more technology to intermediate human interactions, we no longer have to sit face-to-face with one another during uncomfortable conversations. Learning how to be open, honest, respectful, and compassionate with others during difficult conversations is a skill that needs to be cultivated. Unfortunately it seems that technology is hindering our ability to strengthen this skill.

Additionally, the internet allows for anonymity, which means we can say just about whatever we like without consequence. We can say something hurtful without the other person knowing that we were the one who said

---

43   https://newsroom.ucla.edu/releases/is-technology-producing-a-decline-79127
44   https://www.ncbi.nlm.nih.gov/pmc/articles/PMC7967628/
45   https://www.journals.uchicago.edu/doi/10.1086/707985

it. Anonymity online takes the guardrails off of our behavior because we perceive there to be no personal consequence for saying whatever we like. This is not reflective of real life, in which everything we do has consequences. Just because we can't see the consequences of our unchecked behavior on another human being does not mean they don't exist.

Echo Chambers

Lastly, we cannot discuss the impact of technology (and social media specifically) without mentioning echo chambers. Echo chambers are environments where a person encounters only information or opinions that reinforce or mirror their own viewpoints.[46] They are pervasive in online environments as algorithms continually feed us information that will keep our attention for longer – things it already knows we are interested in. YouTube, Instagram, Facebook, Google, and other platforms know what we like to see and so they show us more of the same. The result is that we end up with a very narrow perspective of reality, one that can be heavily based on misinformation or bias. How do echo chambers inhibit our ability to remain open, curious, and compassionate in the face of alternative viewpoints?

The above offers a quick peek into some of the effects of increased technology on our daily lives. It is by no means exhaustive and even within each of these categories, there are additional studies that provide further nuance and understanding about how digital media influences us.

But technology is not going anywhere; it is here to stay. So what can we do to harness the potential that it offers without detracting from our well-being?

Tech and Our Future

> *"Happiness is not something ready-made.*
> *It comes from your own actions."*
> Dalai Lama XIV

As in a previous chapter, we talked about the difference between content and context. In life, we cannot always change the content of our experience, just as we can't change the fact that technology is a central part of modern

---

46   https://edu.gcfglobal.org/en/digital-media-literacy/what-is-an-echo-chamber/1/

society. However, we can change the context – the light in which we see it and the way in which we use it. We can develop a relationship with it that empowers and supports us without enslaving ourselves.

We cannot deny that technology creates plenty of new opportunities for us. It can free up time for us to explore more of what we love, it can help us to work with greater freedom, and it can support us in remaining 'close' to those we live physically far away from. This is the positive side of technology, which exists in contrast to the tendency of addictive behavior or withdrawal from real life that it can create.

There are a few different practices we can explore to help reclaim our agency over how we engage with the digital reality at our fingertips. Consider the following:

1. Bring mindfulness to your online behaviors.

First, it is important to remember that you can't change what you aren't aware of. Often, we deny or avoid the reality of our habits and behaviors because we know that drawing attention to them might lead us to making changes. However, if you truly long for more happiness and wholesomeness in your life, you must be willing to look at what is happening in your life at present.

In the study mentioned earlier that examined the impact of limiting Facebook, Instagram, and Snapchat usage on our well-being, it was also found that both the limited use group and the control group showed significant decreases in anxiety and fear of missing out as compared with baseline. This suggests that just the act of self-monitoring may help to shift our behavior.

2. Establish clear boundaries.

Next, it is important to establish clear boundaries around when technology and what kinds of technology can enter into your life. For instance, prior to the digital era, we could not have fathomed letting the voices of friends, family members, or strangers into our bedroom first thing in the morning. Now, many of us turn to our phones before even crawling out of bed, allowing the thought streams of anyone and everyone online to mingle with our personal energy. If morning scrolling is an activity that you engage in, is this something that could use a boundary?

Get clear about what your boundaries currently are. Do they exist? Then, inquire into what you desire your boundaries around technology to look like – when you will engage with virtual reality and when you won't. When you do engage, how long will you engage for? How can you keep yourself accountable? Asking these honest even if difficult questions can help you to become more conscious and intentional of your actions.

3. Figure out what works for you and what doesn't.

As you continue to mind your engagement with digital technology, become curious about what works for you and what doesn't. For instance, monitor your emotions, your energy level, and your ability to engage with your loved ones as it relates to the amount of time you spend online. Figure out what works for you and what doesn't. You get to consciously decide how much digital disruption you will accept and in what ways.

Furthermore, be on the lookout for nuance in your analysis. For instance, you might find that certain aspects of social media (such as chatting with distant relatives) have a positive impact on your well-being as compared with other features (such as scrolling). Be willing to see things on a greyscale, not just black and white.

Figuring out what works for you requires seeing the opportunities available to you. What are the positive sides of the digital era that you can make the most of? How can you use technology to serve you rather than enslave you?

4. Spark a conversation with your loved ones about the impact of technology.

Lastly, start a conversation with those that you trust regarding your relationship with technology. Every one of us in this digital age is impacted by what we consume online. You might discover that others are also trying to change their behaviors and this open dialogue could create a sense of support and community.

📝 Journal Exercise: Pause for Reflection

To enhance mindful awareness of your relationship to the digital world, consider the following reflection questions. Take your time to sit with these, cultivating curiosity, patience, and self-compassion. Let the insights that arise settle in as you write out your answers in a journal. Given what you discover, how will you move forward from here?

1. How have digital disruptions impacted my personal well-being? How have they influenced my relationship with my family or other loved ones?

2. What do I want more of in life? How does technology support or detract from what I truly yearn for?

3. What do I want less of in my life? What would it take for me to accept less of these things in my life?

4. What commitment or intention can I set today to make technology truly work for me?

The Mindfulness Influencers

I have been involved in training meditation teachers for a fair amount of time. In my experience of different cultures and countries, I have come across a fair variety of participants, ranging from very religious at one end to neuroscientists at the other. However, of late I have seen the phenomenon of "influencers" showing up in my classes. This is new to me, as no one could successfully accuse me of being social media savvy, so it's been a learning curve.

A few years ago, I was about to start a certification program and was told by the organizer that there were some well-known *mindfulness influencers* who had been invited to the program. Given they had a big following of mindfulness-interested people, they could be a good channel to promote future events. I had to admit I was quite intrigued, given it was my first extended exposure to this genre as we were going to be together for 5 days.

Once the class started, on the first day we began to discuss the subject of present-moment awareness. Within the first hour of the class, I realized that the two influencers were continuously on their phone. They would look up to listen to me for a few minutes and then their eyes would be back to their phones, typing away. My first thought was that maybe the content was boring them but it was pointed out to me in the break that they had already posted over 30 pictures from the event. As the day unfolded, I realized that it was not my content or even during inquiry, where they were asking or answering the question, that they would keep pausing to fiddle with their phone. And during our customary sits/practices, they would also sometimes fiddle with the phone.

After the first day, I approached them gently and suggested that their practice would deepen if they were able to keep the phone aside and engage in the inquiry or the practice. They quickly schooled me that they had hundreds of thousands of followers, who kept sending them questions and comments they needed to answer right away so could not afford to not be on their phone for more than ten minutes. And I noticed that even during evening walks, chats, and meals, they were always on the phone!

Wow! Both the meditation teacher and neuroscientist in me could not help but notice that it was almost an unhealthy addiction. What really surprised me was that they were "mindfulness influencers", meaning every day they would post videos about how mindfulness, present moment awareness, etc., were important in life, without embodying any of it. It was even more curious to discover neither of them had any daily practice.

So basically, they were talking and posting about mindfulness and meditation as experts but had literally close to zero practice and embodiment. And a large number of people were following them – much more than other experienced, serious teachers.

As I looked more at their work, I noticed there were some very interesting and unique meditations they were leading on Instagram live for their followers - plant meditation (holding a plant in your lap), wine meditation – meditating while drinking wine (open eyes), feeding the dog meditation, just to name a few.

Maybe I am old-fashioned and too dogmatic in my belief that true present-moment awareness is cultured as you go inwards, experience the space, and allow boundaries to melt. And that, every meditation teacher at the very least must be a regular practitioner and keen student. Demonstrate congruence thereof.

Needless to say, the certification did not work well. The participants (influencers) did not want to commit even to ten minutes a day practice (they were too busy for that) and were unwilling to experiment with one hour – device free/in nature /journaling time.

Maybe it's too much to ask from a digitally disrupted generation.

Footnote: Last month I saw one of them posting in a group about *Netflix binging meditation*. No, I am not joking.

CHAPTER 6

The Six Levels of Happiness

As you begin to inquire about what kind of life you *have* been living and what kind of life you *wish* to live, your understanding of what happiness is or could be will naturally expand. However, there is typically still uncertainty about what it means to truly be happy. What is this experience we call happiness and how can we support its presence in our life?

People tend to think of happiness as an abstract concept with some material or tangible attributes. When unexamined, happiness is believed to be derived from the things that make us feel 'good' or that we *relate* to happiness, such as a particular career, body image, self-confidence, relationships, and so forth. By now, you have likely come to realize that there is more to happiness than the satisfaction that is derived from these external objects or circumstances.

Once we realize that happiness – or well-being or wholeness – is not a product of the things that we attain or achieve in life, we might believe that happiness must be a result of finding meaning or purpose. We tend to hold these aspirational ideas of well-being, believing that there is something we should be doing or that we need to aspire to in order to deepen the experience of innate happiness.

Meaning and purpose are indeed a part of the picture, but this view is still incomplete. To better understand what happiness really is, we can expand our awareness to consider that happiness occurs on a gradient – a gradient that offers us various tastes of what this ideal state of being might be.

The Gradient of Happiness

> *"We are happy when we are growing."*
> Gretchen Rubin

Rather than being a fixed entity or an experience that looks the same for everyone, happiness exists on a gradient. It is a feeling of well-being or wholeness that has a variety of different qualities and it is experienced differently from person to person and also throughout one's life. As we move through life and begin to ask deeper questions about the nature of happiness, we flow along the gradient into more expansive levels of this experience.

We will have a look at the six levels of happiness in a moment but first, it will be helpful to offer a few points of consideration and clarification. First, it is important to note that the journey into broader experiences of happiness is not always linear. Some of these six levels can happen in tandem or we can flow up and down the gradient at different moments in any given period of time. At the same time, like Maslow's hierarchy of needs, we tend to explore lower levels of the gradient to some degree before stepping into new ways of being or knowing happiness.

Additionally, each individual's journey across the gradient will look unique to who they are. Not everyone will have the same aspirations. Innate individual characteristics and life experience (nature and nurture) will shape the path each human takes to discover greater well-being in their life. No person's path is better or worse than another's. Each is simply different.

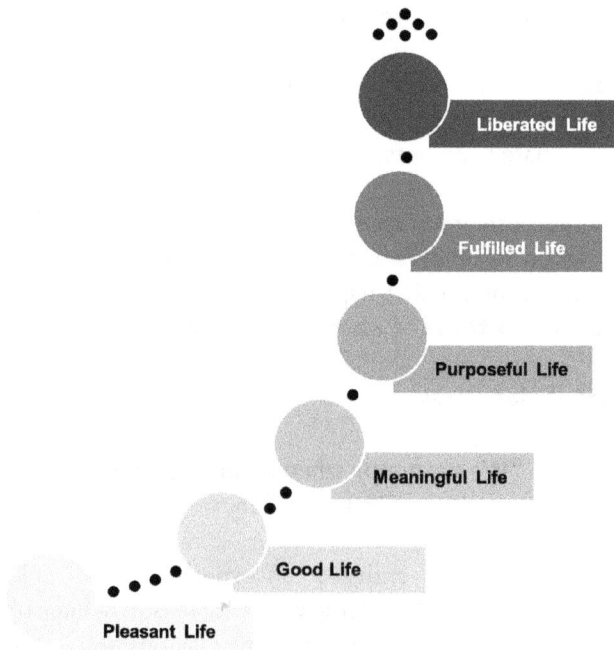

Liberated Life

Fulfilled Life

Purposeful Life

Meaningful Life

Good Life

Pleasant Life

As you explore the six levels of happiness as conceptualized in the image, keep that last point close to heart. We are not here to judge ourselves or others for being 'here' or 'there' on the gradient. The point is to be compassionately mindful of where we are and to take whatever next step awaits us. If we believe that the later faces of happiness are 'better' than where we are now, we will be led to believe that happiness exists only when we reach a certain place or at a later time. Since happiness only ever exists in the present moment, it can only be found or discovered, or experienced wherever we currently stand. It is a way of being, not a fixed destination.

Pleasant Life

At the beginning of the happiness gradient is the pleasant life. Happiness derived from the pleasant life involves primarily hedonic pleasures – joy or satisfaction from the things that we 'like' or 'desire'. If we are living a pleasant life, we likely have all of our basic needs met and are able to enjoy some of life's most sought-after pleasures: good food, entertainment, travel, physical pleasure, and consumer products, to name a few.

Happiness at the level of the pleasant life is not 'bad', but it is limited. It is the form of happiness most strongly associated with consumerism or consumption. As we know, pleasure that comes from outside of ourselves can lead us to become trapped in a cycle of consumption. On the hedonic treadmill, well-being is conditional upon whether or not we 'like' the outer content of our lives and, therefore, it is unstable and short-lived.

Different people respond differently to hedonic pleasures. For some, hedonic pleasures can easily lead to cycles of addiction, whether that be to drugs, alcohol, food, digital media, or something else. Others are able to develop a more harmonious relationship with life's pleasures, which may lead to a different sense of satisfaction at this level of happiness. As a result, the felt and embodied experience of this form of happiness is unique to each one of us.

Good Life

Next is the good life. The good life could also be called the great life, depending upon the degree of contentment one finds at this stage of the gradient. The good life includes the hedonic pleasures of life just as the pleasant life does. However, it also includes a sense of engagement with the world beyond oneself, such as with family or work life. Engagement here refers not to being involved in some external realm of life because one has to be but rather because one enjoys it. For example, an engaged worker is not engaged because she shows up to her job every day. She is engaged when she does so with genuine interest.

We transition from the pleasant life into the good life when we naturally broaden our lens from focusing exclusively on personal needs, desires, and wants to include those of a larger familial or social network. Happiness begins to bubble up within us not just from having one's own needs met but also from realizing the interdependence of the individual within the larger unit. Qualities of sharing and caring blossom at this stage and, again, not because one feels that they 'should' share and care but rather because they naturally wish to.

Most modern psychology, though it may use much more aspirational words, in essence, focuses largely on this level of happiness as it involves strengthening our ability to engage genuinely and authentically with the world around us. Building friendships, showing gratitude, cultivating compassion, and forgiving people from the past are just some of the ways we can increase engagement in our broader familial or social networks. As we do, our experience of this level of happiness expands.

Meaningful Life

Now, it is not uncommon while living a good life to start asking certain questions that you hadn't asked before. We can experience a particular quality of wholeness while still wondering: *Is this the best I can do with my life? Is there something more?*

Other questions that we might start asking at this stage, which signify a step into a meaningful life, are:

- Who am I? Why am I here? Am I living my greatest life?
- What is my purpose? What do I want to contribute with my life?
- How do I get off the fast lane and into a more fulfilling life?
- Am I living as my most wholesome self?

That final question is not just about maximizing accomplishments; it also includes a yearning to expand in order to experience a full range of human emotions. When we start asking what our maximum potential for life is rather than in terms of a single point of focus (i.e. a career or financial success), our hopes expand to include visions of being of service, of pursuing our passions, or of following an inner calling.

All of these questions signify an entry into self-development. There exists a longing to become a better version of oneself and to grow in ways that we could not previously have known about or envisioned. We might not know where we are going or what exactly it is we are yearning for, but deep down there is a sense that there must be more to who we are and to life itself.

The points of inquiry we arrive at while exploring a meaningful life do not always lead to a definitive answer. Rather, insights slowly begin to unfold, helping us to naturally step into a way of being that brings a deeper sense of fulfillment. We crave a relationship to something larger than ourselves, which is what this shift is really about. As a result, it often involves some type of existential awakening or spiritual realization, but it does not have to come in those terms. One does not need to have any spiritual or religious inclination in order to step into a meaningful life.

Purposeful Life

Our capacity for a purposeful life opens up when our pursuits shift in bigger ways – ways that, like the previous level, we could not have fathomed prior to the shifts occurring. Cultural, religious, and professional dogma begin to dissolve and our search becomes less personal. Our desire to find meaning expands beyond what we have to offer to our family or our society. Rather, we become curious about our purpose in the larger unfolding of the macrocosm. We might wonder: *What is the energetic or archetypal role that I play here?*

Our purpose at this stage is not tied up with goals or accomplishments. Neither is it about being a good parent, a good human being, or a valuable contributor to society. It is not goal-oriented, even though it may be driven by particular values. At this stage, we start to view life as a dance – a natural unfolding – and we begin to see our purpose and our place in the world as a part of that. It is no longer about 'I'; it is about syncing into a deeper connection with the rhythm of life in the most authentic and genuine way possible.

Fulfilled Life

Living a fulfilled life occurs when our discovery of what our life is for becomes an everyday experience. In other words, it is when we naturally embody the sense of meaning and purpose that we uncover in the other layers. This level of happiness is reflected in all of our interactions, even the seemingly mundane. When we experience happiness on this level, the existential questions and striving energies subside as we naturally live from a position of knowing our place in the wider web of life.

It is important to note here that a fulfilled life is not a singular endpoint. In other words, meaning, purpose, and fulfillment are not linear; you do not graduate from one before getting an experience of the next. Rather, these three levels of happiness are different layers of the same experience. A blend of them all offers us a complete sense of integration, oneness, and wholeness.

For example, in one moment you might find yourself deeply embodying a sense of purpose in daily life. The next day, you might wake up with more questions than answers about your unique place in the world, embodying more of the 'seeker' way of being. And on another day, you might experience an unraveling of cultural or professional dogma that helps you to step away from everyday goals and into a more integral sense of purpose.

Meaning, purpose, and fulfillment unfold side by side. So, it is natural if you find that you ebb and flow through these different experiences of happiness. These levels are not in competition with one another; in fact, they enhance one another, offering us various tastes or access points to happiness. The same can be true for the pleasant life and the good life; even after you broaden into a life of greater meaning, fulfillment, and purpose, you may still experience the qualities of happiness associated with the first two levels in the gradient, albeit in lesser degrees.

Liberated Life

Eventually, we land at the sixth level of happiness – the liberated life, or a life of embodied wisdom. At this stage, we experience a blend of self-actualization and self-realization (concepts that will be explored in the coming chapter). When our capacity for happiness expands to this level, we experience a sense of freedom and boundlessness. This freedom is not freedom from any perceived social constructs or limitations; rather, it is an experience of being limitless and in harmony with all other sentient beings.

At this level, you make friends with plants, you spend time absorbing the vastness of the ocean, and you appreciate the sun, the air, and all other aspects of existence. When liberated, you are aligned with your purpose, which becomes your duty – but not in the way we commonly use that word. Your purpose is not your duty because it is 'good' or because you think you 'should' take it on; rather, your purpose is your duty simply because 'it is' - it is your personal calling.

Additionally, when we experience this stage of happiness, neither the mundane nor the supramundane are of interest. Quite simply, the true nature of things becomes our greatest interest and curiosity.

The freedom we experience at this stage is freedom on many levels, such as:

- Freedom from the mind that says "I like this" or "I don't like this"
- Freedom from conditioned thinking and ways of being
- Freedom from worldly afflictions, such as jealousy, greed, and craving

The true embodiment of wisdom begins at this stage as you come to realize fundamental truths about life, such as the impermanent nature of all things and the existence of one single macrocosm (within which you experience a sense of oneness and harmony). The wisdom we unfold into here holds two facets: deep, broad thinking, which is often demonstrated by philosophers and scientists, and deep inner knowing, which is demonstrated by mystics and seers. At this level, we are able to hold these two facets of wisdom at once.

This stage is also accompanied by a state of spiritual awakening – a deep realization that helps you to unfold into harmony at all levels of your being. This frees your consciousness from the mundane experiences of life as you become aware of the temporal yet impermanent nature of your human experience. This is different from spiritual seeking in that we are no longer grasping for certain revelations or insights; rather, they unfold quite naturally from our inner being. That being said, if we are in a spiritual seeking phase of our lives, we might catch glimpses of this freedom and liberation when we enter into deeply meditative states of being. These glimpses might inspire us to continue growing and evolving.

Moving Forward & Honoring Your Personal Path

"In a forest of a hundred thousand trees, no two leaves are the same, just as no two journeys along the same path are the same."
Paulo Coelho

So, how do we expand our experiential awareness to encompass more of what happiness can be? This beautiful journey is fueled by our capacity to nurture wholesome and expansive qualities of life, qualities such as curiosity, presence, compassion (for self and others), humility, awe, and wonder. It is also fueled by our commitment to the questions, to our personal practice (i.e. meditation practice), and to the process of discovery.

There are no clear-cut steps to follow as each one of us comes into this life with different predispositions, tendencies, and preferences. We each also have a unique road to follow and lessons to learn. Just as we each have a fingerprint that is unique, so too there is a path before us that is all our own.

This is why self-development is an essential component of stepping into a more meaningful way of living. We cannot bypass the personal; we need to witness it, get to know it, and integrate it with broader truths. Even liberation is not about denying the personal: it is about recognizing it for what it is while also seeing beyond it.

As you start to explore what these different levels of happiness mean to you at this moment in time, consider that happiness is neither abstract nor concrete. It has certain qualities that can be witnessed and cultivated and yet, at the same time, it is not fixed or quantifiable. Think of it in terms of a gradient, knowing that there is always opportunity to expand your felt experience of happiness as you move along the curve. One level is not ultimately 'better' than another in the same way that an orange is not ultimately better than an apple. We can have our personal inclinations (and fruit preferences!) while remaining open to and curious about the other experiences that are possible.

📝 Journal Exercise: Pause for Reflection

Take some time to read through the descriptions of the different levels of happiness outlined above. Then, answer the following questions in a journal. Remember that there are no 'right' or 'wrong' answers to be given. The most suitable answer is what is true for you at this moment. Trust the journey and know that you are right where you need to be.

1. On the left side of the page, write down the names of the six levels of happiness. Next to each level, write down on a scale from 1 to 10 how much each of these levels resonates with where you are right now. A rating of 1 would be given if you do not resonate in any way with the description provided. A rating of 10 would be given if you feel that the description is deeply embodied in each cell of your being.

2. Looking at your ratings, which levels of happiness resonate most with you right now? There may be just one or there may be a few.

3. Of the six levels of happiness, which ones do you feel most strongly compelled to develop at present?

4. What practices can you introduce into your daily life to help you develop these levels of happiness? Remember that you are not searching for the 'right' answer but for what feels true and supportive to you right now.

As with all other journal exercises, you do not have to reach clear answers to these prompts. Sit with these questions for ten to fifteen undistracted minutes, writing down whatever arises. If you need to, set the questions aside and come back to them at another time.

A Monk, a Researcher, and a Greek

I once spent an extended time living at a Buddhist monastery. The abbot of the monastery, whom we respectfully addressed as Bhante, was a very senior monk, who had traveled the world over teaching the true essence of the message of Dharma. One of the unique teachings of Bhante was his focus on 'smiling' while meditating and life in general. He would often say that many meditators do not achieve deep states because their minds are very 'tight', they are too serious (I would totally agree with him on that).

In my first few days of living at the monastery, if I happened to meet him at lunch, he would always tell me to smile more. And slowly, a smile became my most natural facial expression. Bhante's monastery was located in a rural and very conservative area of the USA. When I would go into town to buy some supplies, I would get 'looks' and stares, as people were not used to seeing outsiders, apart from immigrants. Getting back from one of my trips, I asked Bhante what it was like for him to visit the rural conservative Baptist town wearing his Buddhist monk robes. He answered that initially, people were wary, and then they realized that everyone with him was always laughing and smiling, even when they went out to eat. It made them curious and they usually asked him what keeps him always smiling and happy, to which he would answer without hesitation, "*Buddhist meditation – you should try it too*". If you have been to a conservative US town and talked about Eastern meditation, you will appreciate the simplicity and profoundness of this. Simple as it may sound, it was one of the more inspiring moments of my monastic life!

Another instance I want to share is from my travels to Greece. Over the numerous trips I have made to this wonderful country, I made some deep friendships. One of the unique things I have noticed about Greek people is their capacity to be happy on the weekends, regardless of whatever happened during the week. I have seen my friends go through really tough times at work, have deep somber conversations, complain about the government, protest in the street, and then on the weekend join them in a celebratory meal where they are smiling with their whole being as if they did not have a single worry! This is a huge contrast to what I have seen in other countries I have lived in. I once asked a friend, a real estate professional, how it was so effortless for her and her friends to be happy all the time. She responded by saying: "*We are Greeks, this is how we grow up, this is all we know. We are never going to be the richest, or smartest but we try to be the happiest.*" And then she went on to share with me her experience of being married for a decade to a German, where her inlaws were constantly asking her why she was so happy all the time!

I guess from the above two experiences, I learned that in addition to everything else I said in the chapter, happiness does have both "nurture" and "nature" components. And I venture to speculate that by nurturing happiness, we begin to unfold the true nature of ourselves of being wholesome and free!

CHAPTER 7

The Journey from Happiness to Fulfillment

You might be sitting with the previous chapter thinking, "It all sounds great, but how can I actually *experience* those levels of well-being that exist higher up on the gradient? How can I experience true fulfillment?"

First, it is important to note that each person's journey looks different from the next. We each arrive in this present moment and in this life at large with unique experiences, predispositions, conditioned beliefs, and needs. We each have our own path to take that shape shifts as we make our way along it. Additionally, the journey is not a linear one as we've touched on, even though it may appear to be. We might find that we circle our way through a variety of states of being, all the while moving towards expansion of our experience.

In any case, the diagram below outlines the basic journey. We begin by tapping into our full self-expression, which unlocks our capacity for self-actualization and self-realization. Each of these stages or levels includes key elements, which we will take a closer look at.

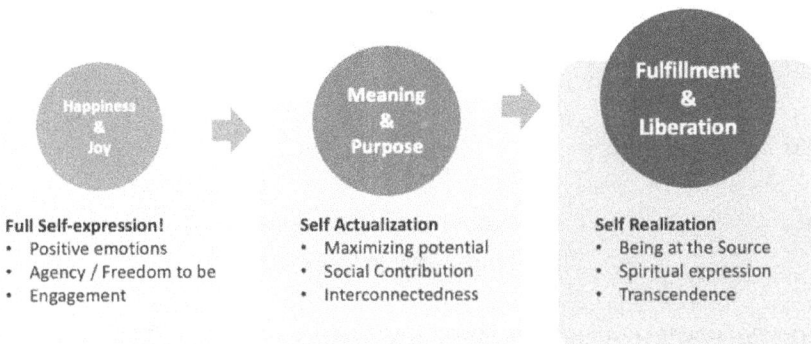

Happiness & Joy → **Meaning & Purpose** → **Fulfillment & Liberation**

Full Self-expression!
- Positive emotions
- Agency / Freedom to be
- Engagement

Self Actualization
- Maximizing potential
- Social Contribution
- Interconnectedness

Self Realization
- Being at the Source
- Spiritual expression
- Transcendence

Full Self-Expression: Happiness & Joy

The journey from our most commonly recognized experience of happiness to deep fulfillment begins with experiencing our full self-expression. It occurs when there is a transition away from unconscious engagement with the hedonic treadmill of consumption. At this stage, we begin to discover what types of feelings we authentically long for and we start to show up for life in ways that honor those desires.

The three core components of full self-expression are:

- Positive Emotions

- Agency / Freedom to Be

- Engagement

The positive emotions we experience at this stage of the journey include peace, vitality, joy, serenity, hope, and inspiration. This list is by no means exhaustive, but it offers a snapshot of what we mean by positive emotions. At this stage, we do not necessarily experience positivity all of the time, but we find that even amidst the storms of life, it becomes easier to return to feelings of inner stability, acceptance, and strength. This develops and deepens throughout our lifetime.

Full self-expression also requires personal agency: the ability to make choices for ourselves and to act independently of others. When we have the agency to follow our inner compass, we can more readily tap into a sense of inner alignment, ease, and well-being.

As Immanuel Kant wrote:

> *"Freedom is independence of*
> *the compulsory will of another."*

We no longer do things because others desire us to or, at the very least, it occurs to a far lesser degree. We recognize that we have the freedom to choose and we no longer give our power over to feelings that say we must do this or that because another person or society expects it of us. If we get married, it is because we desire to. If we have children or if we jump on a new career opportunity, it is because we desire to. Empowerment to make these choices for ourselves fuels joy and happiness.

The third core component of this stage of the journey is engagement. We show up for our job, our family, or our passion projects not because we think we should but because we desire to. We are not detached from the content of our lives, nor are we passively moving with it; rather, we are fully and actively participating in the momentum of life.

To experience greater joy and happiness at this level, we can work on strengthening our capacity for any of these three core elements: positive emotions, agency, and engagement. Again, this will look differently for different people, but some of the actions or inquiries that can support development at this stage include:

- Cultivating and expressing gratitude

- Exploring the genuine needs of body and mind

- Practicing mindfulness, meditation, or any other centering practices

- Discovering and practicing activities that fuel a sense of vitality

- Exploring boundaries and any issues around personal autonomy

- Exploring inner belief systems that work in opposition to joy and happiness (with the support of a professional as needed)

- Exploring personal skills and interests to uncover what genuine engagement would look like for oneself

Journal Prompts for Full Self-Expression

Reflecting on the right questions can facilitate a deeper understanding of what full self-expression might look like for you. Putting pen to paper, take some time to explore your answers to the following questions.

1. What emotions do I wish to experience more of? What actions can I take to cultivate more of these types of experiences in my life?

2. In what areas of my life can I cultivate more agency to engage in activities and ways of being that are in greater alignment with what I care about?

3. What do I enjoy doing? List everything that brings you a sense of fulfillment whether it is related to work or leisure.

4. What patterns of thinking or behavior do I engage in that work in opposition to joy and happiness? List these with self-compassion and without judgment.

Self-Actualization: Meaning & Purpose

The next stage of the journey toward fulfillment is to explore deeper questions of meaning and purpose, which supports the process of self-actualization. As we saw in the previous chapter, meaning and purpose typically coincide with some type of existential inquiry or realization. At this stage, the question becomes: How might I actualize the vision I see for the world and my role in it? This question is at the heart of self-actualization, which in another way can be understood as the manifestation of your dharma (your innate duty) or your life purpose.

The three core components of this stage are:

- Maximizing Potential

- Social Contribution

- Interconnectedness

Fundamental to self-actualization is the maximization of one's potential. However, our 'potential' is not about reaching goals, finishing big projects, or attaining particular outcomes. Rather, it is about reaching your highest potential at all levels of consciousness at which you are awake. This occurs on two life axes: the horizontal axis (the path of mindfulness) and the vertical life (the path of meditation) as reflected in the next diagram.

Path of meditation
(Vertical Life)

Relationship with the Macrocosm
(Shared divine destiny / Purpose)

Relationship with Higher Self
(Spiritual or Soul Purpose)

Greater Life Purpose
(Nurturing your Inner Self)

Family → Work and Social Relationships → Social Contribution → Path of Mindfulness **(Horizontal Life)**

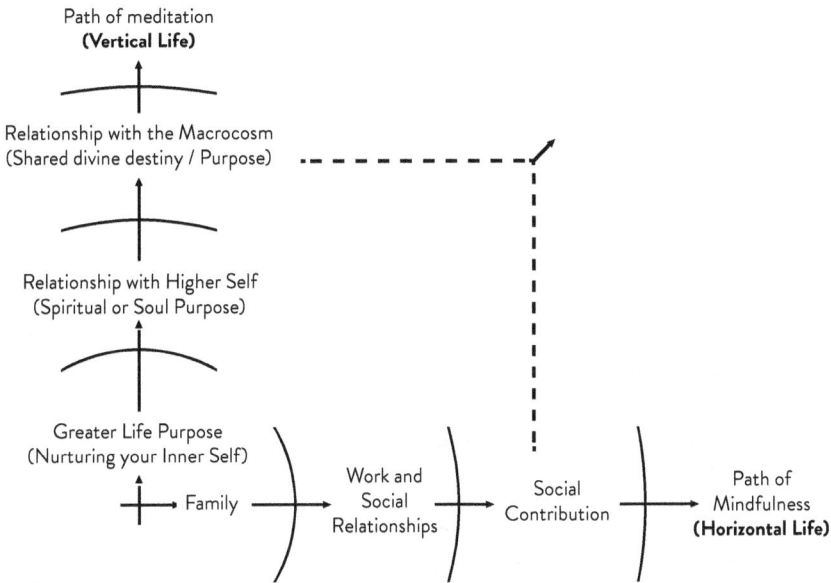

Typically we think about maximizing our potential in terms of what happens in our career or in some other area of life that we deem most valuable or worthy. However, as we look at this diagram, we can start to ask questions about how we can maximize our full potential for being in areas and aspects of life we are not so accustomed to exploring.

Social contribution, the second core element of this stage in the journey, is seen on the right-hand side of the horizontal axis. One of the key signs of being able to explore deeper meaning and purpose undoubtedly comes when we question how our life expression impacts those around us. How do we want to live as a social citizen? How can we serve the area in which we live and the people who live all around us? These questions begin to come naturally as we realize that a fulfilling life is not just about us; it is about supporting the well-being of the wider web.

This drive towards social contribution ties into the realization of our interconnectedness. We come to recognize that, even though we are autonomous beings with free will and agency, we are innately connected to all other beings. How we show up in the world has a ripple effect, which we begin to recognize. Awareness of how we engage with others and with life at large comes into full view and we begin to find motivation and inspiration in values such as kindness and compassion.

On exploring the themes and questions that arise as we step into this next phase of our journey, we come to realize that what unfolds is directly related to what we see as the boundaries of who we are and what we are here for. While our awareness expands along both the horizontal and vertical axis, so too does our potential.

At this stage, we can further our growth through a variety of contemplations and actions, such as:

- Engaging in self-inquiry, which requires a willingness to ask often difficult questions

- Further assessing personal strengths, resource availability and considering how these serve the community at large

- Practicing compassion-based meditation, such as metta meditation

- Increasing awareness of personal biases, fears, and perceived limitations

- Reframing what it means to 'maximize our potential', expanding out from previous assumptions

- Taking action (in whatever way one feels drawn to) that supports the well-being of others

📝 Journal Prompts for Self-Actualization Enquiry

To deepen your capacity for self-actualization, consider the following questions. Sit with them in contemplation for as long as you need to and then write down your reflections in a journal. Know that you can come back to these questions anytime that you wish to and that you do not need to arrive at a 'perfect' or clear answer.

1. What does my community need that I have the skills and interest in providing?

2. What ideas do I have about what my sole purpose might be? In other words, what might my unique self be uniquely designed and destined to cultivate, share, or offer to this world?

3. Referencing the diagram that outlines the horizontal and vertical axes of personal expansion, what parts of each path require more of my attention?

4. What personal fears, biases, or limiting beliefs might be inhibiting my capacity to maximize my full potential in service of the wider web of life?

Self-Realization: Fulfillment & Liberation

As you continue the journey of expansion, there may come a time when your sense of self shifts from a personal 'me' to a universal 'I'. In other words, the limited egoic identity becomes more translucent as we recognize that everything is a part of the dance of life – ourselves, our emotions, and our thoughts all included. Nothing is ultimately personal or belongs to 'me'.

Self-realization, which offers deep fulfillment and liberation, occurs when we tap into the completeness of this dance – of this oneness. Oneness, which is often taken to mean that "everything is one" (a true statement in a sense), can more accurately be described as "nothing left out." When we experience self-realization, everything is on the table, everything is welcome, and we enter into a state of deep acceptance and flow. There is a harmony discovered between the microcosm of our own lived consciousness and the macrocosm of the universe.

The three core elements of this stage of the journey toward fulfillment are:

- Being at the Source

- Spiritual Expression

- Transcendence

First, there is this sense of being at the source of life rather than being separate from it. At this stage of awareness, we come to realize that we are experiencing life in a vessel but that we are *made* of life. Since we are at the source of life, we recognize our potential and power to create. Life does not just happen to us (though of course, things happen beyond our control.) However, we begin to see ourselves as a co-creator of our existence.

This awareness of being at the source of life often comes hand in hand with spiritual realization and expression, the second component of self-realization. This looks differently to different people. Some might understand spiritual expression through concepts and words of a particular religion, be it Christianity, Buddhism, or another. Or, one might have their own words and ways of understanding or expressing themselves as a spiritual being. In any case, the words and concepts matter little; those are just the external clothing. What lies at the core of spiritual expression and awakening is a sense of or belief in the ultimate energetic mystery of life.

At some point, whether after years and years of exploration or in an unexpected flash of insight, we might find ourselves at a point of transcendence. Transcendence, a concept that may seem elusive or confusing to some, is simply what occurs when we move beyond our cognitive understanding of spirituality or our personal expression of it. It occurs when we naturally uncover a depersonalization of everything that happens in our life. In a grander sense, nothing happens to us or for us. It simply is.

It is important to note that we do not have to experience transcendence in order to live a fulfilling life. As expressed in the previous chapter, happiness, and well-being will look and feel different for each one of us. There is no 'right' or 'wrong' way to go about the journey. In fact, it is better to take your own journey rather than the path you think you 'should' take or what others are taking.

To explore your capacity to expand into greater degrees of fulfillment and liberation, consider the following steps forward:

- Studying ancient texts and traditions that speak to you

- Developing a daily meditation practice

- Making a commitment to your personal evolution and self-study

- Prioritizing the activities that nourish your soul or spirit

- Examining personal fears, aversions, attachments, and cravings

📋 Journal Prompts for Self-Realization Enquiry

Self-realization is not something that we can think our way into, but at the same time, reflecting on big questions can support us. As with all of the journal prompts in this book, there are no 'right' conclusions that you need to come to. Simply allow the questions themselves to broaden your sense of curiosity and openness to the mystery of life.

1. What is your understanding of God, the Universe, the mystery of life, or any other sense of a higher power that you resonate with? In other words, what is your sense of the life force that lives in all of experience?

2. What spiritual, religious, philosophical, or other wisdom teachings speak to or inspire you? If you are unsure, where might you find resources to expand your awareness of life's energy?

3. What daily action or practice can you commit to for the next 30 days that will help you to expand spiritually or energetically or that will help you to experience a deeper connection with all that is?

Trusting the Process of Expansion

As you explore each of these three stepping stones of the journey toward liberation and fulfillment, remember that this does not have to be a perfectly linear progression. In life, we often circle around and around certain experiences, practices, and lessons until the glimpses of insight and meaning we encounter take root in a more embodied way. Your path may include highs and lows, which is a part of being human. Practice patience, curiosity, and self-compassion as you move further into this work.

Furthermore, always remember that you do not need to be anywhere in particular on this roadmap. One stage is not 'better' or 'worse' than another. In any moment, we can support our journey by wholeheartedly accepting where we are and by trusting that, from an expanded sense, life has perfectly shaped our journey for us. You are always where you need to be and you can take the next step from where you are.

The components that make up self-realization, such as transcendence and the recognition of being at the source of life, can take forever to arise or they can happen in an instant. In either case, once you expand into greater levels of insight and understanding, you cannot lose that awareness. Though it may be a journey of learning how to embody the wisdom or clarity that you've gained, you are always expanding. Trust in this process of expansion and you will find that surrendering to it comes more effortlessly.

In the next section, we will move into a more thorough exploration of how to nurture the seeds of happiness, well-being, and fulfillment. Concepts and practices such as gratitude, goodwill, forgiveness, and conscious meaning-making will be brought into greater light to support you in unfolding your greatest expression and experience of life.

So What – Then What – Life Is

A successful entrepreneur, Nikos, was invited by a friend to attend a lecture by a spiritual teacher. For about an hour, the teacher waxed eloquently about the need to focus on spiritual growth. Toward the end of the Q&A time, Nikos asks the teacher, "Why is spiritual growth important?" The teacher responded, "It helps you realize the importance of service and bring forth a greater sense of fulfillment."

Nikos was initially intrigued but, although he did not know what to do with it, felt there was more he needed to learn about the subject. As his curiosity grew, he started reading more spiritual books and became well-versed in Eastern mysticism and philosophy. He attended a few more lectures and retreats and began to feel an internal change that made him want to go to Asia for a true immersion in the culture.

Soon the opportunity came up and he boarded a flight to Nepal. On the plane, he was sitting next to a gentleman who was listening to music on his Walkman. When the meal was served they had an opportunity to talk and Nikos asked his fellow passenger why he was going to Nepal. He received a response that the man was going to visit some local art galleries that he once exhibited in and that he constantly travels to countries, finds work locally for a few months, and then moves to another place. On being asked for the purpose of his own visit, Nikos explained in detail his own journey of having discovered Eastern spirituality and how important it is for growing. Nikos was happy that he had found an audience and continued to educate his neighbor on the flight about the benefits of meditation/spiritual learning, etc.

Soon he was peppered with child-like curious questions from his fellow passenger about how Nikos felt that he was growing, what he had learned, and what he intended to do with it. Nikos soon proudly confided that he wanted to be a yogi, as they have an inspiring presence, to which he was asked, *"So what? What is so special about being a yogi? Can you not be inspiring without being a yogi?"* Nikos was a little upset with the question and responded that if he becomes a yogi, it would allow him to achieve deep states of meditation and potential enlightenment. His neighbor pressed further by asking, *"Then what? What would you do after enlightenment?"* Nikos didn't like the question at all but, out of courtesy, he replied that he would have a great life and that maybe his fellow passenger should try it too so he can understand how great a life it is when you arrive at enlightenment.

By this time, his fellow passenger had realized that Nikos was perhaps feeling a bit restless so he quietly said, *"Thank you my brother for sharing this wisdom with me. For I am yet like a child, that believes life is just whatever is happening inside me. But then I have not read as many books as you."*

Nikos closed the conversation by suggesting that it was never too late to start and that he could always share some pointers over coffee if they met in Nepal. The neighbor thanked him, and closed his eyes, quickly drifting into sleep. On arrival at the airport, they parted ways and Nikos was a little surprised when his neighbor told him that he did not have a phone number or email address. *No wonder this man has no roots or a plan of life,* Nikos thought to himself.

Two weeks later, Nikos was invited by the abbot of the monastery he was staying at to an event where a greatly renowned teacher was delivering a talk on "Yoga of Immortality". The event was being held in the local city palace as some members of the royal family were also students of the speaker. Nikos excitedly arrived early at the venue and sat in the front row. Soon the speaker, along with the royal family host, walked on stage, in a dress that looked like that of a zen teacher. He looked vaguely familiar to Nikos. The first words out of the speaker's mouth were, *"My brothers and sisters, life just is. It's not somewhere you are trying to get to in the future, it's not what you have lived already. It's just that moment you are now living. Even immortals live life one minute at a time. So today I am going to share with you how you can experience this minute as eternity – this is the yoga of eternity".*

Nikos sat in stunned silence. He had recognized this voice – it was the voice of the passenger that sat next to him on the flight. And soon, tears were streaming down Nikos' face. He knew he had found his teacher, and he was home.

As always, this is a true story with names changed, but this time I will share a little more personal context as this story is very close to my heart. As I say in my classes, while I can neither confirm nor deny, there is a chance that in the real life, the teacher might have been **Shifu** – one of my teachers who taught me the science of breath, and Nikos may have been my Brazilian friend, who first introduced me to him, but what matters is to remember Shifu's message: Life just is – a moment in time, a breath, a footprint in the sands of time. And to have realized that unfolds the greatest of freedom! Freedom of life itself!

SECTION 3

Nurturing the Seeds

You now have a map that outlines the journey through expanding and ascending levels of happiness. This map provides a variety of questions and considerations that will support your personal growth. We will take a closer look at much of what has already been covered as foundational to your journey of expansion in this next section, that is, nurturing the seeds of positive emotions.

The seeds of positive emotions – or of well-being – include things like gratitude, the will to do good, forgiveness, self-healing, and conscious meaning-making. Some of these might appear relatively simple or obvious at first glance, but most of us know that being grateful or doing good or offering forgiveness (as examples) are not always easy or a given. In this section, we will explore how these seeds of positive emotions nurture us, along with how we can welcome them more integrally into our experience – even when times get tough.

CHAPTER 8

Gratitude

Most of us are familiar with the practice of gratitude. Whether we already practice it or not, it is not uncommon to hear people talk about giving thanks before a meal, keeping a gratitude list, or counting their blessings. Gratitude is not new and yet many of us do not give it the attention that it deserves.

You might also have heard that gratitude is good for you. Instinctively, we can sense this to be true. If we feel appreciative of various things in life, we are probably more likely to feel good. The correlation is intuitive. But can gratitude be learned? And, what impact does it really have on our body and mind? Let's explore the findings behind the claims that 'gratitude is good for you'.

Gratitude on the Mind-Body Vessel

> *"Gratitude unlocks the fullness of life. It turns*
> *what we have into enough, and more. It turns denial*
> *into acceptance, chaos to order, confusion to clarity."*
> Melody Beattie

To understand how gratitude impacts us on various levels, we first need to consider what constitutes the mind-body-energy vessel. We often hear about the relationship that exists between body and mind, but what does this really mean and what does it have to do with gratitude?

The mind-body vessel is the name for the union between what you experience on a mental-emotional level and what you experience as your physical body. Without giving it much thought, we often think that the mind is one thing and the body is another, but the reality is that what happens in one of these realms has a direct impact on the other. They are more fused as one than they are separate.

Think about what happens when you become stressed. Thoughts such as, "I am not prepared for this presentation," or "What will happen if I don't meet this quarter's goals?" can lead to both an intensification of emotions as well as a physiological response. Stress hormones increase and energy is diverted to skeletal muscles and the brain. Research also shows that cells in our immune system become activated.[47]

Modern science is also beginning to understand and explain how the physical body can store past trauma and memories, although much is still left to be discovered. When we have an experience that we are not able to metabolize, this accumulated energy becomes stored trauma. The experience is 'remembered' by or 'stored' in our fascia, which is a thin layer of connective tissue that surrounds all of our organs, bones, muscles, blood vessels, and nerve fibers. It contains nerve endings, which makes it sensitive and responsive to stress, under which it tightens.[48]

Myofascia is a term for the subset of fascia that surrounds our muscles. It is said that this tissue, which contains many sensory receptors called interoceptors, can stimulate areas of the brain that control our emotional state.[49] This suggests that mind-body communication is a two-way street – our mind and emotions impact our body (through stress) and various states or positions of the body can impact the mind.

This understanding of the mind-body as one single system rather than two distinct parts can help us to grasp just how important nurturing the seeds of positive emotions are – seeds like gratitude. When considering the impact of gratitude on the totality of the mind-body vessel, we can frame our understanding through three unique contexts:

1. Gratitude allows you to cultivate positive emotions.

The first and perhaps most intuitive positive impact of gratitude is its impact on our perspective and emotionality. By cultivating feelings of thanks and appreciation, we strengthen our skill to see the 'good' that exists in our life, rather than focusing on what is so-called 'wrong' or 'bad'.

---

47   https://www.ncbi.nlm.nih.gov/pmc/articles/PMC2568977/
48   https://www.hopkinsmedicine.org/health/wellness-and-prevention/muscle-pain-it-may-actually-be-your-fascia
49   https://www.karger.com/Article/Fulltext/464149

Gratitude helps to shift the lens through which we view the world. For instance, it enables us to see a rainy day as a gift to the earth, even if our plans were canceled or we were hoping for a day at the beach.

Gratitude also helps to boost levels of dopamine and serotonin in the brain.[50] This is a physiological change that shows up on an emotional level since these two neurotransmitters support feelings of contentment and can boost our mood. Research has also found that those who are more grateful (as compared with those who experience less gratitude) also experience greater life satisfaction and hope, along with reduced depression, envy, and anxiety.[51] One study that showed an increase in life satisfaction in accordance with higher levels of gratitude found that as life satisfaction increases, so too does gratitude, which creates a positive, reinforcing cycle.[52]

This seed of positive emotions also supports us in opening up to a more boundless way of experiencing life. Without gratitude, we may take our blessings for granted, and yet, the more we tune into what we can give thanks for, the more beautiful and rich life becomes. This shift of perception also helps us to develop a new relationship with our difficulties. On the surface of our experience, a challenge (whether that be a health challenge, a relationship difficulty, or something else) may appear to be a 'negative' experience. With a foundation of gratitude beneath us, we are able to approach our challenges with greater receptivity to lessons and silver linings. This is not always easy, but with practice, we can start to uncover hidden teachings and gifts that underlie all of our experiences.

2. Gratitude opens a door to healing and physiological well-being.

Additionally, gratitude is a doorway to healing and physiological well-being. In understanding the mind-body connection, we understand that what happens on a mental and emotional level leaves its mark on the physical body. During gratitude practice, neurological pathways

50   https://www.psychologytoday.com/us/blog/comfort-gratitude/202012/gratitude-is-gateway-positive-emotions
51   https://www.researchgate.net/publication/279403394_Gratitude_in_Practice_and_the_Practice_of_Gratitude
52   https://www.frontiersin.org/articles/10.3389/fpsyg.2019.02480/full

and somatic experiences are triggered that allow us to heal in ways that modern science doesn't yet fully understand.

Some of the physiological changes that have been observed through gratitude practice include:

- Reduced levels of cortisol, the body's stress hormone[53]

- Reduced markers of inflammation and increased heart rate variability[54]

- Increased brain activity in the medial prefrontal cortex, an area of the brain associated with empathy, feelings of relief, and emotion regulation[55]

- Increased dopamine and serotonin, as referenced earlier

Studies have also found that gratitude is a predictor of post-traumatic growth.[56] Following traumatic events, gratitude enhances resilience and reduces depression.[57] Furthermore, one study that examined the connection between gratitude and PTSD symptoms among Israeli youth exposed to missile attacks found that gratitude may function as a protective factor against post-traumatic stress through its ability to increase appreciation of life.[58]

Gratitude has also been shown to improve sleep, support our relationships, and boost feelings of optimism and generosity.[59] All of these benefits combined support us in healing on both physical and mental-emotional levels. Gratitude can thus be seen as a balm for mind and body, wired together through the nervous system and other pathways that support internal communication.

53   https://positivepsychology.com/neuroscience-of-gratitude/
54   https://greatergood.berkeley.edu/article/item/can_gratitude_be_good_for_your_heart
55   https://www.mindful.org/what-the-brain-reveals-about-gratitude/
56   https://www.ncbi.nlm.nih.gov/pmc/articles/PMC6901784/
57   https://ggsc.berkeley.edu/images/uploads/GGSC-JTF_White_Paper-Gratitude-FINAL.pdf
58   https://www.tandfonline.com/doi/abs/10.1080/17439760.2014.927910
59   https://www.psychologytoday.com/us/blog/compassion-matters/201511/the-healing-power-gratitude

3. Gratitude supports and nurtures other virtues, such as benevolence and altruism.

Additionally, gratitude is often considered to be the 'mother virtue' due to the immense power it holds not only to impact well-being but also in its ability to impact our embodiment of other virtues. As the mother virtue, it supports the cultivation of things like benevolence, altruism, and forgiveness.

This may be because gratitude, as mentioned, shifts the way we perceive the world. 'Negative' events become 'challenging' events, which become opportunities to learn and grow. As our lens of perception shifts, we draw different conclusions about people, systems, and situations, becoming more willing and able to see the good in all things.

Altruism, for example, becomes more readily available to us since we naturally develop a desire to care for things that we see the good in. Forgiveness, too, is easier when we are able to see more goodness in other people, despite what may have happened between us. Generosity flourishes in the presence of gratitude as well since gratitude helps us to shift from a lens of lack to one of abundance and blessing. It has also been found that gratitude, when trauma is present, can help individuals find meaning as they interpret their life to be a gift.[60]

These are just a few examples of the virtues that blossom in the presence of gratitude. Ultimately, this mother virtue helps to open our energy field, shifting us out of a contracted state of being to a more expansive one. This creates the space we need for all forms of goodness to grow.

> *"Wear gratitude like a cloak,*
> *and it will feed every corner of your life."*
> Rumi

Three Levels of Gratitude Practice

If we feel that we could use more gratitude in our lives, the best step forward would be to practice it. We might have preconceptions about what gratitude

---

60   https://www.ncbi.nlm.nih.gov/pmc/articles/PMC6901784/

practice looks like, but it can help to first consider that there are three different levels of gratitude practice, all of which are worth engaging in.

The first stage of gratitude practice is to feel gratitude. We cannot move into a more advanced gratitude practice without genuinely knowing what this energy feels like. Despite what some might believe, feeling gratitude is not something we need to (or should) sit around and wait for. It is a frame of mind that we can train and we do so by tuning into the many gifts we have been granted.

Daily gratitude rituals (explored further below) are one way to begin feeling a sense of gratitude. Whether practiced first thing in the morning, at midday, before a meal, or even at the end of the day, developing a daily gratitude practice helps to train our brain to sense into what we have to be thankful for. It is often too easy to overlook the gift of electricity, water, or our loved ones if we have not learned to appreciate it. In other words, if we are not conscious of what is good in our lives, it is easy to take things for granted.

Another practice to enhance the feeling of gratitude is visualization. Through visualization, we can call to mind someone who has helped us in our life – perhaps even someone who has since passed. This practice can help us to re-experience the positivity that was bestowed upon us by the goodness of another while also reminding us that we are connected and supported. Additionally, if we visualize ourselves offering our thanks to this person, it can help us open up to the next level of gratitude practice.

This second level is that of expressing gratitude. It is one thing to feel gratitude and it is another thing to openly share it. Expressing gratitude unlocks another level of the experience of this virtue. It offers us the chance to deepen our connection with that person or thing we are grateful for. When expressed to another person, not only does it boost our own well-being, but it also enhances theirs, thus creating a collective field of positive emotion.

One of the most common ways to express gratitude is through letter writing. A 'gratitude visit' is a practice not just of writing a letter of appreciation but also of hand delivering that letter and reading it aloud to the recipient (outlined further below). In Chapter Four, we highlighted a study conducted by Dr. Martin Seligman. In this study, participants that wrote and delivered a letter of gratitude showed the largest positive changes of five different gratitude interventions. The boost in happiness was maintained at the one-month follow-up.[61]

The third practice of gratitude, which also involves the cultivation of gratitude, focuses on tapping into gratitude when times are difficult. Paired with breath awareness, this practice can help to induce the parasympathetic nervous system response, thereby reducing stress or panic and increasing feelings of wholesomeness. This can be easier said than done, but taking small steps into a greater capacity to feel gratitude during times of difficulty can enhance our resilience and inner stability.

To strengthen this skill, we first need to remember to tune into the breath when we find that we are overwhelmed by stress. Slow, steady breathing with long exhalations helps to stimulate the vagus nerve, which triggers the relaxation response.[62] Once we have eased the experience of stress, we can practice the ten fingers exercise – counting out ten different things in our life that we are grateful for at this moment. If this feels like too much at any given moment, we can remain focused on the breath until we feel grounded. Then, we can start by just noting one thing we are thankful for – perhaps the breath itself, maybe the ground beneath us – and then seeing what we can expand our awareness to include.

---

ayam™ TIP

Gratitude is one of the most powerful practices of mediation in the ayam app. This has a direct correlation with improving quality of life, especially reducing stress and enhancing vitality. I recommend this practice before going to sleep!

---

61   https://www.researchgate.net/publication/7701091_Positive_Psychology_Progress_Empirical_Validation_of_Interventions
62   https://www.ncbi.nlm.nih.gov/pmc/articles/PMC6189422/

Practice: Four Gratitude Practices to Enhance Well-being

The four gratitude practices outlined above are explained in more detail below. Explore these practices at your own pace, considering making a commitment to one per week over the course of four weeks. Observe how each one shifts your perception, your state of being, the state of being of others around you, and your relationship to various people and situations in your life.

1. The Gratitude Ritual

Choose a time of day to develop a gratitude ritual – a three-minute journal process of writing out all that you are grateful for. You might choose first thing upon waking, during your lunch break, before going to sleep, or some other time of day that suits your schedule.

Set a timer for three minutes or simply note the time on the clock as you begin. For the next few minutes, write a list of everything you feel appreciative of. You could begin with present-moment blessings before expanding to include blessings in your day as a whole and then blessings of your life at large. Engage in this practice for a minimum of one week.

2. The Gratitude Visualization

Find a quiet place where you can sit or lie down for ten minutes undisturbed. Call to mind someone in your life that has assisted you in some way, whether this person is alive or has since passed. You may or may not still be in contact with this person.

Once you have a person in mind, envision yourself sitting in a comfortable place with them, expressing all the reasons that you are grateful for their presence in your life. What did they gift you with? How did they support you? Let them know exactly how you feel and observe what impact this has on you and on the version of them in your mind's eye.

3. The Gratitude Visit

Call to mind someone you are grateful for that you can visit in person within the coming week. It may be someone you live with, someone who lives nearby, or someone who you have plans to meet up with soon.

Once you have chosen this person, take out a piece of paper and a pen and begin to write them a letter. Express to them all the things that you appreciate about them. If they inspire you, explain why. If they have supported you in some way, express what this meant to you.

When you meet with this person face-to-face, read the letter aloud to them before gifting them the letter to keep. Note what this experience is like for you and for them. How does it shift your connection? How does it shift your well-being and theirs?

4. Ten Fingers Exercise

During a difficult time when you sense a strong need within yourself to relax, to tune in, ground your energy, and broaden your perspective, gift yourself with a few moments of pause. If possible, find a quiet place to sit still for at least three to five minutes.

Begin by taking five to ten long, slow breaths, letting the exhalation be slightly longer than the inhalation. Once you feel settled, inquire:

Despite the challenge or difficulty I find myself in,
what am I thankful for?

Begin naming your blessings, however small or large, as you count them out on your fingers. Depending on the degree of difficulty you find yourself in, there may be some resistance. Acknowledge any resistance with patience and compassion and continue to breathe until your inner capacity for gratitude is able to recognize something it is thankful for. Keep breathing and keep noticing, listing your blessings until all ten fingers have been counted.

Journal Prompts for Self-Realization Enquiry

To further cultivate a sense of gratitude for increased well-being and healing, work through the following journal prompts. Some of these questions might also be well-suited for a daily gratitude ritual.

1. Who is someone in your life at present that you are thankful for?

2. How does it feel to consider expressing your gratitude for them in a letter to be hand-delivered? If there are inner barriers to this idea, what are those barriers and how might you overcome them?

3. Name a past difficult situation or experience in your life that you once perceived as 'negative' or 'a problem' that you now see as a blessing or opportunity. What do you see now that you could not see then?

4. What is one inner resource or gift that you are grateful to have within you?

5. Amidst moments of difficulty, what is one thing you can always be grateful for?

Adversity and Gratitude

Boris is a neurosurgeon, whom I have known for a few years. He usually has a very high opinion of himself and often treats most people around him as "less accomplished". This was most noticeable to me in the way he would tell the nurses that worked with him that they "always needed to listen to him as he had 12 more years of education than any of them".

Additionally, he is quite rich, which means he has a lifestyle that many can only dream of – private jet and multiple holiday home type. This made him a firm believer in the idea that 'money was a good barometer of how smart someone was'.

After one particularly awkward conversation during which I saw him berate a colleague, I gently suggested to him that he should be a little bit more humble and that he has many blessings in life he needs to be more grateful for because not everyone is as blessed.

He snapped back at me, saying, I had a "Crunchy socialist mentality," and that he had not received any help in his life to get where he is and, hence, he didn't owe the world any humility. For obvious reasons, I did not see him very frequently and only met him again recently after almost three years.

I was pleasantly surprised to see his transformation. He had developed a very kind style of communication, and a lot of humility. After about thirty minutes of observing him, I could not stop myself and said, *"You have changed. What happened?"*

He replied, *"If you are a neurosurgeon and get a stroke, you realize none of your knowledge can help with recovery. You notice the compassion and competence of your colleagues looking after you and you are totally dependent on them. Especially when you feel helpless in the ICU, what you remember most is a nurse holding your hand, when she recognizes you and says you will get better, that you have many lives to save. How can you not realize how little you matter, and yet how much you have left to do? I am so grateful to be alive. That I can breathe is enough for me to feel grateful."*

So just in summary, if you are alive, you can breathe, if you have your health, your family, it's more than enough to be grateful for every day!

CHAPTER 9

Goodwill and the Will to Do Good

Rooted in the same principles but not the same, *goodwill* and the *will* to do good are two important seeds for nurturing positive emotions. They are interrelated and yet that does not mean a person necessarily embodies them both automatically. Both virtues are rooted in kindness and positive intention, but the will to do good includes an additional component: committed action.

One is not more important than the other, but for either to reach its full expression, it needs its counterpart. They are mutually nurturing: goodwill provides the will to do good with authentic, loving intention and the will to do good provides goodwill with expression – with action.

Let's take a look at how these two seeds can be more deeply understood and what it takes to nurture them – including when it feels difficult to do so.

Establishing a Foundation of Good Will

> "*The ideals which have lighted my way, and time after time have given me new courage to face life cheerfully, have been kindness, beauty, and truth.*"
> Albert Einstein

If goodwill and the will to do good were put in sequence, goodwill would come first. Goodwill is the foundation of positive action, but it is more about intention than anything else. Goodwill is more common than the will to do good and that is because it is typically easier. We'll get to the difficulties of 'good action' soon, but in the meantime, what is goodwill really and how can we nurture it?

Goodwill, often described as a feeling of benevolence or kindness, is our intention for goodness in this world. It is the genuine wish for well-being for another person, for an animal, for an ecosystem, for a community, or for any other system, the planet as a whole included. Understandably, it establishes a foundation for us to be more conscious citizens of the world.

Having this positive intention for the well-being of others is the foundation of positive, helpful action. Intention always comes first. It is not the same as 'doing good,' but it is certainly the right place to begin creating a more beautiful world – for others and for ourselves. One study, for instance, looked at the impact of simply wishing others well, finding that looking at others while thinking, "I wish for this person to be happy," improved the participants' sense of care and connectedness.[63] It also found that this form of loving-kindness (not involving any other type of action but intention) reduced anxiety and increased happiness.[64]

We all experience goodwill to varying degrees. In some moments, it rushes through us quite naturally, such as when we see a loved one suffering. In other moments, it can feel out of reach, such as when we feel hurt or angry. Our capacity for goodwill is not fixed, and like other virtues, it can be nurtured and strengthened.

It is also helpful to note that though goodwill is a virtue in and of itself, it relies on other virtues for support. For instance, non-judgment, altruism, harmlessness, and compassion are virtues that support our capacity to experience goodwill. If we are judgmental, it is hard to remain connected with care and well wishes for another. If our intentions and actions are self-serving or contain ill intent, it will be equally difficult to experience genuine goodwill. Additionally, if we struggle to feel compassion for another person, we cut off the source of our goodwill, making it almost impossible to truly wish another person well, particularly if we are in disagreement or at odds with the person in question. As we nurture these supporting virtues, goodwill is deepened, layer by layer, and we find ourselves with an increased capacity to wish the best for others.

These virtues, including goodwill itself, can be strengthened through a variety of practices or meditations. Goodwill comes from Anahata and Vishuddha, the heart and throat chakras (energy centers) respectively, according to ancient Vedic understanding of the energetic system within

---

63   https://www.medicalnewstoday.com/articles/324843#The-effects-of-12-minutes-of-loving-kindness
64   ps://link.springer.com/article/10.1007/s10902-019-00100-2

the body. Practices that focus on increasing and balancing the energy that flows through the heart and the throat can support us in untangling any barriers we have to goodwill and in reconnecting with our compassionate heart center. Metta meditation, for instance, is a practice of cultivating loving-kindness. Practices focused on increasing awareness of our shared humanity can also be helpful.

We can also enhance our embodiment of goodwill through simple, everyday practices. When you meet someone you love, try taking a moment of silence to wish them well. Then, see if you can extend this practice to acquaintances, strangers, or even people you have difficulties with. Over time, your natural inclination towards goodwill will grow.

You can also consider the presence of goodwill in the workplace. Often, workplaces are rife with competition, which inherently puts us 'against' others. However, when we invite the quality of goodwill into our interactions, competition can transform into collaboration. In practice, this might look like starting morning meetings with a quiet wish for everyone in the workplace to thrive rather than focusing on how we as an individual will succeed. Alternatively, you might practice a formal goodwill meditation each morning. Explained in further detail later in this chapter, this is a practice of imagining the entire workplace ecosystem thriving – including each and every individual that it is comprised of.

Cultivating the Will to Do Good

As we are establishing a more concrete foundation of goodwill inside ourselves, we can also consider what it takes to actually *do* good. The will to do good is our willingness to put in the energy required for positive action. Sometimes this comes naturally to us, but doing good is not always easy. Often, the 'right' thing to do sometimes requires prioritizing another's needs above our own, even if temporarily. When this happens, we might find ourselves having to swim against the tide of self-interest in order to take positive action.

For full engagement with the world, we need to find ways of taking that step from positive intention into the domain of action. Thinking or talking about doing good can be a valid place to start, but action helps goodwill transform from an idea or ideal to a tangible experience that supports someone or something else.

Though the will to do good should be selfless (that is, not based on a desire to get some kind of return on our energy exerted), it is still worth noting some of the research around taking positive action to help others. One study found that spending a greater amount of one's income on others predicted greater happiness.[65] Additional findings suggest that acts of kindness can increase feelings of self-worth, reduce blood pressure, and increase endorphin production.[66] The love hormone oxytocin and our feel-good chemicals dopamine and serotonin can also increase through acts of kindness.[67]

So how do we take that leap from positive intention into action? Where do we start? While cultivating the foundation of goodwill is centered around nurturing the virtues related to goodwill, the will to do good grows when we focus on the 'will' aspect of our behaviors. Will, which has a variety of definitions, includes not just the intention to do something but the determination or choice to actually do it. In order to have strong will, we must be willing to work against any forces (conscious or unconscious) that hold us back from the positive action we wish to engage in.

There are various levels of will. Emotional will is our strength to remain calm and balanced. Mental will is our capacity to stay rational and logical. Spiritual will is our ability to stay on the path regardless of any distractions that threaten to pull us off it. Physical will is the physical vitality we embody to carry on. As we work on strengthening our will at all levels, particularly where we feel that we struggle, we create a fabric of emotional, mental, spiritual, and physical strength to support our positive engagements in the world.

To start working with our will, we can first take a close, honest, and compassionate look at those inner barriers we have against doing good and at the levels of our will that are not as strong as they could be. This is not about judging ourselves or making ourselves 'bad' or 'wrong' for having resistance to taking positive action; rather, it's an invitation to get curious.

---

65   https://pubmed.ncbi.nlm.nih.gov/18356530/
66   https://www.dartmouth.edu/wellness/emotional/rakhealthfacts.pdf
67   https://www.cedars-sinai.org/blog/science-of-kindness.html

We might ask ourselves: Is it difficult to follow through with my intention to do good? What makes it difficult? What layers of my will are not as strong as they could be?

Once we are aware of what inhibits us from taking more positive actions in the world, we can start to work with it. For instance, perhaps we hold an unconscious belief that there are just not enough resources (i.e. time, energy, or money) to take the action we wish to take. Can we acknowledge this belief without making it right or wrong? Then, are we willing to consider ways of working through it? For instance, perhaps we also hold a belief that small actions don't make a difference and since we don't have the resources to make big waves in the world, we might as well not do anything at all. Is this belief true? Can it be unraveled further?

Or perhaps we come to realize that our emotional will is not as strong as it could be and that this lack of strength in our emotional will is holding us back from engaging fully with the world. Once we realize this, we can start to inquire about what type of self-care or intervention we might need for healing and strengthening at this level. The same inquiry can occur at any level of will.

Furthermore, another important way to increase our propensity to take action is to simply take action. This might sound difficult if we lack the motivation, but might we consider that action itself builds the motivation and energy for more action? We often sit and wait for action-oriented impulses to arise, but often it is action itself that fuels the impulse to meaningfully engage with the world. One step leads us to another.

Taking action can come in the form of a single, random act of kindness. In fact, random acts of kindness are one of the best exercises to express goodwill and to bridge the gap between goodwill and the will to do good. As you engage in some type of random act of kindness (outlined in greater detail below), notice the impact this has on the receiver of the act, on yourself, and on anyone around you. How do any drawbacks of doing good compare with the benefits?

When the Going Gets Tough

> *"Where people of goodwill get together and transcend their differences for the common good, peaceful and just solutions can be found even for those problems which seem most intractable."*
> Nelson Mandela

During times of difficulty, maintaining goodwill and the will to do good becomes more challenging. When we are feeling triggered, judgmental, fearful, or angry, our sense of separation heightens and we can find ourselves in protection mode. This protection mode, which we might understand as the stress response or fight-flight-freeze mode, can become chronic, holding us in a perpetual sense of separation and making it difficult to engage effectively with the rest of the world.

It is not 'wrong' or 'bad' if we find ourselves here, but it can be helpful to recognize what is happening and ease the stress response so that we can come back to the bigger picture. If we are facing imminent danger, we must of course tend to that first. However, if we are finding that there is no true threat before us and, that rather, we have become stuck in separation or fear, we can use a variety of tools to help soothe the nervous system – to bring us back to our inner stability. These tools can include (among other techniques) mindfulness of breathing exercises, body scan practices, or mindful movement.

Easing the stress response, especially when chronic and in response to no real threat, can help us to remember that we are connected. It can help us open up to the world, feel increased gratitude, and consider where we can actively engage in positive ways. Working with stress and whatever other internal resistance we might feel towards goodwill is far more effective and authentic than forcing ourselves to 'think positively' or to 'be a good person.' When forced, we risk falling even further out of alignment. Only through self-healing, self-inquiry, and caring for ourselves can we authentically and sustainably share our time, energy, and resources with others. Note, however, that doing good for others and doing the work on ourselves can occur in tandem.

Goodwill and the Will to Do Good Practices

In the sections above, I briefly referred to a few different practices that can help us to nurture goodwill and strengthen our will to do good. Three of those practices are outlined in greater detail below: a practice for increasing awareness of our shared humanity, the random act of kindness exercise, and the morning goodwill meditation.

1. Shared Humanity Meditation

This practice, which is a modified version of the Just Like Me[68] practice by Ram Das and Mirabai Bush, can serve to remind us that we are fundamentally more alike than we are different. It can also help to reduce judgment and increase a sense of care, which help to nurture goodwill.

To practice, come to a comfortable seated position, softening your gaze or closing your eyes. Take a few mindful breaths and then call to mind someone that you have mild to moderate difficulties with. Start with someone with whom you have minor difficulties and as you grow increasingly familiar and comfortable with this practice, you can build up to using it with people you feel more at odds with or separate from.

Once you have this person in mind, imagine this person embodying their essence, whatever that means to you. Once you feel connected with an image or sense of them, repeat the following statements while giving yourself enough room to feel into each one:

- This person has feelings, thoughts, emotions, and needs, just like me.
- This person has experienced both physical and emotional suffering, just like me.
- This person has fears, hopes, and dreams, just like me.
- This person longs to be happy and healthy, just like me.

If you wish, you can go through this sequence of statements a second or third time. Then, close your eyes if you've had them open to read

---

68   https://www.spiritualityandpractice.com/practices/practices/view/27782/
just-like-me-compassion-meditation

and envision yourself offering well wishes to this person. When you are finished, come back to your breath and then open your eyes when you are ready. Notice how you feel.

2. Random Act of Kindness

You have probably heard of the random act of kindness practice prior to reading about it here. It is a practice of performing simple, unplanned acts of kindness for friends, loved ones, or strangers. The intention is for these to be 'random', but it is also okay if you become aware of an action that you can take later in the day or week.

To practice, set an intention in the morning to do something good for someone today. You do not need to strategize or figure out what this will be; simply begin with the positive intention.

As you go through your day, keep your awareness open for ways in which you can bridge the gap between intention and action – and take that action when you see an opportunity. There are many ways you might bridge this gap, such as by purchasing or cooking a meal for someone, buying coffee for the person behind you at your local café, inviting your employees to finish work a half hour early, or asking someone who is having a difficult time how you might be able to support them.

After each act, take some time to reflect:

- What was the impact of the action on the receiver?
- What was the impact of the action on me?
- What was the impact of the action on any bystanders (if applicable)?

Commit to one act of kindness per day for one week and at the end of the week reflect on the following questions:

- How did this week of random acts of kindness impact me overall?
- How did this week impact the community or world at large?

3. Morning Goodwill Meditation

To help shift the energy of competition in your workplace to that of collaboration, you can practice a morning goodwill meditation daily. This practice will help to solidify your intention of seeing well-being made possible for all.

Whether you practice this at home or when you arrive at the office, find a quiet place to sit for five minutes where you can close your eyes. Settle in through a few rounds of mindful breathing. Once you are grounded, call to mind the faces of at least a half dozen people that you work with. Include people you are personally close to as well as people you are not that close to.

As you hold these people in mind, you might imagine standing in a circle with them or you might imagine a web of energy interconnecting all of you. This web might extend out to other people as well, perhaps customers or business partners.

As you hold this image in your mind, quietly repeat the following phrases:

May all individuals within this ecosystem be happy, healthy, and successful.
May this web as a whole be happy, healthy, and successful.
May all stakeholders, near and distant, be happy, healthy, and successful.
May all beings that I encounter today live this day in peace and harmony.

Note how this shifts the way you engage with others. After a week of practice, consider the overall impact that this practice of cultivating goodwill has had on you and others.

---

ayam™ TIP

Goodwill Meditation in the ayam app is one of two meditations that I recommend to everyone. Best practiced in the morning, it brings a tremendous amount of flow in life and also invisible prosperity of harmonious human relations.

📓 Journal Prompts

To take a deeper dive into goodwill and the will to do good, consider the following reflection prompts. Write out your answers to these questions in a journal and remember that none of these questions are designed to evaluate how 'good' you are. Rather, they are simply an opportunity to deepen self-understanding and discover where there might be room to grow.

1. In what areas of my life do I have goodwill?

2. In what areas of my life is it difficult for me to extend kindness or well wishes to others?

3. What is it about this situation or relationship that makes it difficult for me to cultivate goodwill?

4. In what ways am I being challenged to grow in this situation or relationship?

5. What practices could help me expand my capacity for goodwill?

6. In what areas of my life do I have the will to do good?

7. Where I am not taking action on my goodwill, what actions would be in alignment with the intention?

8. What inner barriers make it difficult for me to express goodwill in action?

9. How can I overcome my inner barriers to taking action for the good of another?

10. What is one action I can take today to do good in the world?

Hands that Pray, Hands that Serve

While traveling through India, Clarissa a spiritually curious seeker from Canada and a nurse by training, came across an "Ashram" in the holy city of Varanasi. She decided to stay there for a while to study with the charismatic teacher who was the resident monk in the Ashram. One month led to another and before she knew it, she had been in residence for three years. One early morning, the teacher asked her to see him after the morning meditations.

In her audience with the teacher, he asked her about her experience over the last three years. Once she had finished speaking, the teacher further asked, how was she now going to take this back into the world outside and be of service. She did not have an answer and he suggested that she not rush into finding one, but to take some time to meditate on this.

This proved to be a true turning point for Clarissa and she could not sleep all night. She had been searching for inner peace all her life and answers to her existential questions. She felt she had found them all in the spiritual practices of Hinduism and she was home! Why, then, was her teacher asking and in turn implying that she has to go back to the world that she had run away from?

The following morning, she saw the teacher again. Seeing her troubled look, he invited her to another private audience. Before she could speak, he told her, *"There are two types of hands in the world: ones that pray and the other ones that serve. The first is not more spiritual than the other. The greatest expression of spirituality is service. It's the second that makes a lasting difference in the world. Find in your heart what is the purpose of your hands."*

Today back in Canada, she runs a network of schools for indigenous children with special learning needs, allowing them to remain immersed in their cultural practices as they learn to navigate the world of developing employable skills. Her schools are called Hands that Serve and are supported by the church her family has been a member of for several generations. Right at the entrance of each school is the picture of her teacher who she credits as being the spiritual father of the Hands that Serve.

CHAPTER 10
Love and Compassion

What is love really? And what does love have to do with compassion? Are they the same or is there a difference? Just like goodwill and the will to do good, love and compassion go hand-in-hand. As we nurture one, we support the growth of the other, and yet there are indeed differences between them.

Love comes in a variety of shades; like many things in life, it exists on a gradient. From platonic or romantic love to a love that simply embraces the true nature of things, we can think of love as a diverse, nurturing garden. With many flavors to savor, love provides us with a wide array of positive emotions.

Compassion often coincides with some of the flavors of love, and yet interpersonal love is not required for compassion to arise. The highest form of love, however, which we will get to in a moment, indeed supports feelings and expressions of compassion. It helps us to embrace the natural order of things, thereby enabling us to have greater compassion for all beings.

Let's take a close look at these two seeds of positive emotion, exploring how we can support them in coming to bloom.

The Highest Form of Love

> *"Love is the most powerful energy in the universe."*
> Albert Einstein

We are all familiar with worldly love in one form or another. Children, animals, friends, family, or nature at large can evoke strong feelings of care and affection. We love those who are close to us, either platonically or romantically, and while we might describe this love differently, chances are we experience it much the same. Love spurs joy, connection, and warmth.

We talk a lot about love in our modern culture – about finding love, falling in love, and even falling out of love. We crave love and we also fear love because we feel that love can break us. At the same time, there is a higher form of love that cannot be broken – a love that is not conditional upon any particular outcome. This is the highest form of love, a love we might refer to as divine indifference.

The best way to understand love as divine indifference is through metaphor. Think about the sun and the earth. Each day, the sun rises to nourish the plants, animals, and people living upon the earth. It shines its light to bring warmth, nurture food, and simply light up our lives – and it does all of this without expectation. The earth does not turn to the sun to say 'thank you' and yet the sun has no concern with this. The sun keeps burning brightly, not reliant upon acknowledgment to do its job. It shares its gifts – its love – simply because it is its dharma. It is its duty.

This highest form of love is not affectionate, platonic, or romantic. It is simply a commitment to divine duty. The sun embodies this love in its own way, and though we don't typically think of love in this way as humans, it is the highest form of love for us as well. To experience this most expansive energy field of love is to commit ourselves to our personal dharma or the natural order of things.

To conceptualize the journey toward divine indifference, consider the following roadmap. This is the evolutionary matrix of love:

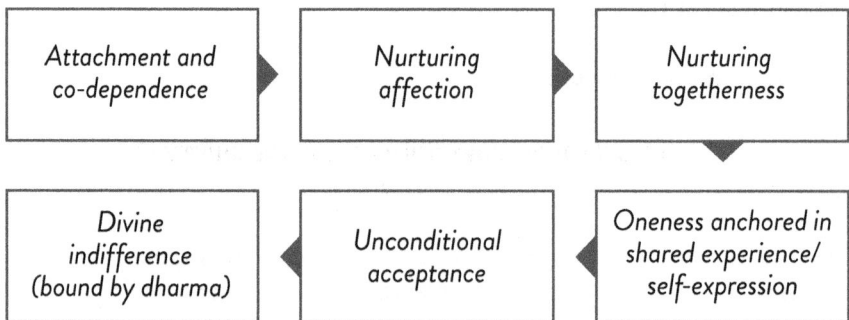

Attachment and co-dependence	▶	Nurturing affection	▶	Nurturing togetherness
Divine indifference (bound by dharma)	◀	Unconditional acceptance	◀	Oneness anchored in shared experience/ self-expression

At the beginning of the path, we find the forms of love we are most familiar with: a sense of attachment, feelings of affection, and a sense of being a unit. This sense of being a unit might eventually expand to a greater sense of universal oneness (albeit with a shared, personalized experience) before growing even wider to include unconditional acceptance. Once we are able to experience unconditional acceptance, our final step is into divine indifference – into a love that honors things as they are.

Unconditional acceptance and divine indifference may sound quite similar, but there is a key difference. When we experience unconditional acceptance, there is still an element of the personal. We might think something along the lines of, "I really want that promotion, but I will extend acceptance to the outcome regardless." With divine indifference, there is the added element of surrender and the absence of personal desire. We are more deeply committed to things as they are as compared to how we wish them to be. We do not try to accept; we simply do.

When we talk about divine indifference, it is not uncommon for resistance or misconceptions to arise. We might think that divine indifference means not caring about things, and therefore we might reject it. However, being committed to the natural order of things does not mean we forget our humanity. Compassion and concern for the well-being of others still exist even as we relinquish our personal desires for things to be this way or that way.

In fact, as we awaken to the level of divine indifference, we naturally embody greater love, care, and concern for the well-being of others. This is because love is a cosmic principle present in literally all sentient beings. Plants, the soil, bees, birds, rivers, forests, and oceans are all imbued with the cosmic principle of love – love in its highest form. As our understanding of love expands to this universal level, our sense of separation or being 'different from' dissolves.

Separatism, hate, and jealousy are all learned behaviors that have become more embedded in societies as they have moved from being collectivist to more individualistic in nature. This includes animal societies as well. These feelings arise from a feeling of being 'separate from' or 'other than.' Even positive developments, such as the shift from community-focused to family-focus, have also contained a move from oneness to separateness as they have triggered some degree of protectionism.

All of this is to say that hate, jealousy, and separatism are not endemic to our higher nature. As we open ourselves up to more expansive forms of love, the illusion of separation begins to dissolve and we recognize the cosmic principle of love that is woven through each and every one of us. In this way, divine indifference supports us in loving and nurturing all individual beings (the personal) and also recognizing life's natural order (the universal) and the divine duty we hold within it.

The Power of Compassion

"Compassion is the wish to see others free from suffering."
Dalai Lama

Compassion, on the other hand, may be inspired by the universal principle of love, and yet it operates on the personal level. It is something we extend to others and that others may extend to us. We might consider compassion to be the feeling that arises when we are met with another's suffering and when we feel the desire to relieve that suffering.[69] Compassion reminds us of our shared humanity (or our shared sentient existence when met with the suffering of a non-human being such as a forest, ocean, or animal).

As a virtue, compassion is a powerful one. When we practice it, it helps to further soften the illusion of our separation. Even in the face of differences, we begin to see the underlying current of similarity between us and another. Separatism, hate, and judgment soften and we increase our capacity to exist in more harmonious relationships with people of different backgrounds and beliefs.

Unlike the more common forms of love, one does not need to 'like' or be in any type of relationship with another person to feel compassion for them. We can feel compassion for any being, regardless of our connection to them and regardless of how 'similar' or 'dissimilar' we may be. Our acquaintances, strangers, and even our 'enemies' can be recipients of our care and concern. Unconditional acceptance and divine indifference can support us in strengthening our ability to offer compassion to all, even where it is challenging to do so.

It can also be noted that compassion includes the care we are able to extend to our own suffering. In fact, compassion is not complete without self-compassion. Self-compassion is not self-indulgent and it is not about taking

---

69   https://greatergood.berkeley.edu/topic/compassion/definition

our own 'side' if we find ourselves in conflict with another. It is simply the practice of turning towards our own suffering with the same kindness and well wishes that we would extend to those that we love.

It is important to note that compassion is not about condoning or approving harmful actions by others. In other words, we can have compassion for someone who has hurt another without agreeing with or denying their actions. Compassion, which is fueled by recognition of the fact that we are all made of the same thing, simply helps us to see the suffering and the humanity of another. Compassion does not dissolve our personal boundaries and it can also be fierce. For example, if we've been hurt by another, fierce compassion helps us to uphold our boundaries and to speak for our needs without seeking to punish or harm. The motivation for engagement becomes love and truth, not punishment or revenge.

Saying this does not make it easy to practice compassion during times of difficulty. If we find that compassion is out of reach, we can take a pause to turn inwards. Can we first offer ourselves compassion? Can we first offer ourselves the love, support, and nurturance that we need?

If or when we return our thoughts or attention back to the person who has hurt us, it can be helpful to tap into love as a cosmic principle inside all of us. This does not excuse harmful behavior, but it might help us to realize that the person before us is made of the same thing that we are. It is a big paradigm shift to hold this paradox of the pure love that we all are alongside whatever actions or 'sins' one might have exhibited. This takes practice, but if we can learn to hold this paradox we will find that space for compassion (again, sometimes fierce) begins to grow.

Ultimately, the power of compassion arises because it is fuelled by love. In fact, love and compassion are two sides of the same coin. Love is the substance that we are all made of and compassion is the personal expression of recognizing this fundamental shared humanity. Love is the genesis – the source – and compassion creates the warmth and safety that others can be held within. When we anchor in love, compassion grows. When we practice compassion, our practical understanding of love deepens.

Cultivating Love and Compassion

There are many different practices to nurture the seeds of love and compassion. The shared humanity meditation outlined in the previous chapter is one such exercise. Additional practices are outlined below.

1. Metta Meditation

Metta meditation, or loving-kindness meditation, comes from Buddhism. Metta bhavana (from the Pali language) means 'love cultivation'.[70] It is a practice of cultivating kindness and well wishes towards others.

To practice, find a comfortable place to sit where you can close your eyes for ten to fifteen minutes. Settle in through a couple of minutes of mindful breathing. Once you feel centered, call to mind the following people/groups one by one, in sequence:

- Yourself
- Someone you love
- An acquaintance
- Someone you have difficulties with
- The world or your community at large

Hold the essence of each of these people/groups in your heart and mind (each one individually). For each, repeat the following phrases:

- *May I/you be loved.*
- *May I/you be safe.*
- *May I/you be happy.*
- *May I/you be at peace.*

Take your time offering these wishes to each individual before moving to the next. Notice if this practice shifts anything for you.

---

70   https://thebuddhistcentre.com/text/loving-kindness-meditation

2. Self-Compassion Practice

If you find that you are struggling to hold compassion for yourself, take ten to fifteen minutes to sit in quiet contemplation. Begin by settling the nervous system through a few rounds of mindful or deep breathing. If you feel called to, you might take a few clearing breaths through the heart.

Once you are as settled as possible, note the presence of your inner critic. This is the side of you that is struggling to have self-compassion; it does not represent the entirety of you. Can you witness this voice from the point of view of an observer?

Notice what happens as you watch the inner critic. Often, it softens on its own as the light of awareness is shone upon it. Whether this happens for you or not, shift into self-support by asking one or both of the following:

- *What do I most need in this moment that I can give to myself from within?*
- *What would I offer to someone I love if they were experiencing these same thoughts and feelings?*

Grant yourself whatever you need in this moment to realign with the energies of love and compassion. Once you are ready, take your time to transition out of the practice. Notice how it felt to support yourself.

3. Mindfulness of Bias & Fears

Minding our personal biases, fears, judgments, and negativity is another way to cultivate love and compassion. All of us hold thought patterns and beliefs that keep us feeling separate from or judgmental of others; awareness of these thoughts and beliefs can help us to soften these inner barriers to love.

You can practice mindfulness of bias and fear on an informal basis by taking stock of when you say or do something that is not compassionate. Without self-condemnation or judgment, become curious about what happened. What sparked this behavior? What thought or belief underpinned it? What fears are present beneath the surface in relation to this situation? Inquire with self-compassion, knowing that all actions that are out of alignment with love are wonderful learning opportunities and chances to grow.

4. Committing to the Highest Form of Love

Finally, you can also strengthen your embodiment of love in its divine sense by committing to it. Each morning, take a few moments to sit in silence and internally express your desire to align with your dharma and with the natural order of life. Make a commitment to align with the will of the Universe or of God (whatever word you might use to describe existence itself).

There will undoubtedly be moments when you veer off-course, especially in the beginning. That is okay. Do not expect perfection. Simply make that commitment each day, trusting that the intention and continued practice will support your growth.

---

ayam™ TIP

ayam features Love and Compassion meditation which I personally find is one of the building blocks of inviting in positive emotions, healing, growth, and peace in life. I invite you to practice it with your family and loved ones.

Journal Prompts

Just like all the other themes covered in this book, journal prompts exist for nurturing the qualities of love and compassion. Take your time to move through these prompts, harnessing curiosity and self-compassion as you do.

1. Looking at the evolutionary matrix of love (the roadmap presented earlier in this chapter), what levels of love do you currently experience? What is the next step in your love journey?

2. How can you support yourself to take this next step? What practices or actions would help you to expand your experience of love?

3. What type of love do you *want* to experience? What does this experience require of you?

4. What might fierce compassion look like in practice? What might it feel like?

5. Write a letter of love and compassion to your current self from the perspective of your future self. What words of support, kindness, and care would you offer to the person you are today? What would your future self want your current self to know?

Falling in Love and Freedom with Compassion

Let me share a story about someone from my life, a close friend who we can call Jay. Growing up, Jay had been a bit of a loner and always longed for friendships but they didn't always come easy to him as he was very nerdy and started working at an early age. This made relationships hard for him, having little time to nurture them and not much in common with his peer group. Life brought him much success in most areas except relationships, until he met Cindy, the love of his life, in very unusual circumstances of a missed flight-layover scenario. They had a lot in common, became good friends, lived in the same neighborhood, and quickly moved in together. In Jay's world, he had found his soulmate, and he was the happiest he had ever been in life. It seemed natural and easy – what Cindy would call 'flow'. Was great for a while until, one day, Jay realized that Cindy had been seeing her past boyfriend for a while and had lied to Jay about it. He was understandably hurt and angry, and confronted Cindy. And then something completely unexpected happened – she told him that she never had romantic feelings for him, she pursued the relationship because she felt safe with him and didn't want to lose his friendship. Now, she wanted to explore a relationship that had more romance but had not decided with whom. She didn't want to go back to her boyfriend but desired the space opened for her to explore other relationships.

Jay's first reaction of anger quickly subsided and the feeling of hurt gave way to one of rejection. As time went by, Jay realized that Cindy had been in a series of romantic dalliances with a number of her 'friends', including those they had in common, while living with Jay and projecting to all their social circle that they were a committed couple. For Jay, this now added the feelings of 'feeling stupid and blind' to the ones of rejection, pushing him into a reactionary spree of self-destructive behavior, only to be confronted by his friend who was a therapist. Once he confided in her, she asked him to seek therapy.

Jay also confided in me once he was already in therapy and doing better. I was very shocked to hear the story, especially since I had known the couple for about a decade, and they were the archetype of a 'perfect couple'. I asked him how he was doing and his response will always stay with me. He said, *"It still hurts, I still love her but I recognize that she just loved me differently and perhaps not enough. I realize what she did was right in her mind. My love for her makes me feel angry and hurt. But my compassion for her wishes her well, encourages me to let go, forgive her, and move forward. I am waiting for my compassion to finally transform my love into healing and I will be free."*

Love and Compassion are like the light and warmth of the sunlight. You can't experience one without the other arising with it and touching you. To have true light of peace in life nurturing both is important. The greatest love in life is *Self-Love*, and the greatest expression of compassion is *Self-Compassion*. While Jay may not have got the definitions quite right, I can feel that he is beginning to experience self-love, probably for the first time in his life.

CHAPTER 11
Forgiveness and Self-Healing

Like the sets of pairs explored in previous chapters, forgiveness and healing are two sides of the same coin. This entangled pair supports us in releasing the past, experiencing personal growth, and discovering a sense of freedom. Though forgiveness and self-healing are not always easy or immediate, they are fundamental to our well-being journey.

As you approach this chapter, consider that (like other seeds of well-being) forgiveness and self-healing are not all-or-nothing. They exist on a continuum. This consideration helps to remove self-judgment and unrealistic expectations, enabling us to take the next step in our personal journey from wherever we currently stand. Where forgiveness and healing are sought in our life, we do not need to arrive at 100% forgiveness or be 'completely healed'. These misconceptions about the journey can hold us back from growth. Instead, note where you are and consider where there might be room to expand and grow.

From Forgiveness to Freedom

> *"We must develop and maintain the capacity to forgive.*
> *He who is devoid of the power to forgive*
> *is devoid of the power to love."*
> Martin Luther King Jr.

First and foremost, forgiveness is a pathway to freedom. It offers us the freedom to move forward and to choose where we go from here. Where resentment and blame keep us tethered in the past, forgiveness enables us to look toward the future. Given whatever may have happened, the question becomes: What now?

There are many reasons we might not feel ready to forgive. We may not know how to forgive or we might think the other person involved is not deserving of our forgiveness. We might not feel finished with our difficult emotions or could be attached to a sense of us being right and the other wrong. Whatever the case may be, taking a closer look at our resistance to forgiveness is a worthwhile pursuit given that forgiveness can help us to heal and to move forward.

Another reason we hold back from forgiveness is because we misunderstand it. Many people mistakenly believe that forgiveness is the same as saying "It's okay what happened." Others believe that forgiveness can only occur when we're ready to forget. However, forgiveness is not about condoning harmful behavior nor is it about forgetting whatever may have caused the original hurt. Rather, it is an act of generosity – to both the other person involved and to ourselves.

This is because while forgiveness may help the other party involved to release any guilt they may be feeling for their actions, forgiveness is also an act that supports our own interest – our own well-being. When we choose to open up wider to forgiveness, we are deciding to relinquish our grasp on the story – the memory – wrapped up in our suffering. To choose forgiveness is to grant ourselves permission to grow. It is a step into greater acceptance – not acceptance of the action that stirred the suffering but of the simple fact that the situation happened or that the hurt occurred. This type of acceptance is about choosing not to argue with reality and acknowledging that the past cannot be changed.

Forgiveness has other observable benefits for our well-being. Since chronic anger triggers the stress response, holding onto our hurts with anger or resentment can lead to reduced immunity, cardiovascular issues, and even depression.[71, 72] Research has found that making the effort to forgive can help to reduce anxiety, depression, major psychiatric disorders, risk of heart attack, mortality rates, pain, and stress while also improving sleep and cholesterol levels.[73] Thus, forgiveness is indeed associated with healing.

Again, it is important to remember that forgiveness is not about forgetting. We may still remember what happened, but the memory no longer triggers anything within us. It is also not something we either do fully or not at all

---

71   https://www.hopkinsmedicine.org/health/wellness-and-prevention/forgiveness-your-health-depends-on-it
72   https://www.apa.org/research/action/immune
73   https://www.apa.org/monitor/2017/01/ce-corner

– and we don't go from 0 to 100 instantaneously. Rather, forgiveness is an expanding spiral of acceptance and letting go. We might start off with just a small inner knowing that forgiveness is possible and then slowly, as we nurture seeds of strength, resilience, goodwill, compassion, gratitude, and generosity, our heart naturally expands to a greater capacity for forgiveness. We don't have to quantify our forgiveness, but to paint a picture we might imagine that we start at 2% forgiveness, eventually reaching 25% forgiveness, and then continuing to expand this feeling until the memory of the original hurt holds no charge at all. Eventually, not only is the charge gone, but we might also find that we wish nothing but the best for the other person involved.

We've talked a lot about forgiveness of others, but sometimes the forgiveness needed is that which is self-directed. Holding anger towards or excessive self-criticism of ourselves can contribute to feelings of depression, anxiety, feelings of worthlessness, and self-harm.[74] A lack of self-forgiveness keeps us tethered in the past just as resentment held against others does. Can we find it in our hearts to open up lovingly to ourselves, to accept our mistakes and challenges, and to embrace the fullness of our humanity? As we offer this to ourselves, we might find it easier to offer forgiveness to others as well.

It is also important to note that forgiveness is something only we can do to free ourselves. Sometimes, we hold back forgiveness because we are waiting for an apology, but an apology is not necessary for forgiveness to occur. Rather, it is an internal process and does not depend on anything outside of ourselves. Consider, for instance, where the person we wish to forgive has passed on. It is easier then to see that forgiveness cannot be conditional upon an apology. The question then is: What needs to shift in my own being to move deeper into forgiveness and in the direction of freedom and healing?

Our Capacity for Self-Healing

> *"The wound is the place where the Light enters you."*
> Rumi

Forgiveness plays its role in healing, but healing requires us to expand beyond the lens of forgiveness as well. Self-healing requires that we bear witness to our inner world and that we work towards the transformation of all that

---

74   https://www.goodtherapy.org/learn-about-therapy/issues/self-criticism

holds us back from well-being. Healing works on our traumas – conscious or unconscious – and indeed, we have all experienced some form of trauma.

Before we take a closer look at trauma, it is important to recognize that healing can only ever arise in the self. Therefore, self-healing is the only form of healing there really is. If we long for something to heal (i.e. a habit, an attitude, a memory), it will heal as the inner realm of the self heals. This self-healing transmutes karmic knots, which transforms not just our own experience and reality but also the experience of all those who we are karmically connected to or entangled with. Thus, our own self-healing has a ripple effect on the lives of others.

But returning to this universal experience of trauma: what is it exactly? Many of us don't realize we've experienced varying degrees of trauma in our life because we hold preconceived notions of what trauma is. Many imagine trauma to be something that only occurs when there is a very obvious distressing event in one's life. However, one explanation of trauma that can help us to recognize the less obvious forms present in our own life comes from the addiction expert, author, and speaker Gabor Maté:

> *"In line with its Greek origins, trauma means a wound— an unhealed one, and one the person is compelled to defend against by means of constricting his her own ability to feel, to be present, to respond flexibly to situations."*[75]

Maté also notes that "...trauma is not what happens to a person, but what happens within them." Thus, the situation does not necessarily dictate whether trauma has occurred; rather, we can determine if a trauma has occurred based on the impact of something on our inner world. Subtle yet persistent anger directed at a child, for instance, can create trauma, as can being bullied at school or losing a close grandparent as a child. Trauma indeed comes in many degrees.

A traumatic situation can often be recalled, but it does not always leave a memory. For instance, trauma at the time of birth, falling down the stairs as

---

75   https://www.hoffmaninstitute.co.uk/trauma-resilience-and-addiction-hoffman-inter-views-dr-gabor-mate/

a child, or societal conditions during our upbringing can all leave their mark without our conscious recollection of what happened to us.

Other traumas might be easily recalled, and some traumas might be remembered but their impact is not consciously connected to how we experience life. For instance, Covid-19 is a collective trauma inflicted on our social psyche. We may not recognize the impact it has had on us, but it has undoubtedly shaped the way we view things and how we engage with others.

Even if we cannot recall a particular traumatic event, the event and its impact leave an impression within the body. Thus, we might say that the body remembers things that the mind cannot. This stored experience manifests on various levels of our being – psychological, psychosomatic, psychospiritual, and physiological – and impacts our thoughts, beliefs, emotions, actions, reactions, and other behaviors.

Working with trauma is imperative to self-healing. It is important to recognize that any traumatic experience we have had, however drastic or subtle they may be, limits our expression and experience. As we work on our traumas, we begin to relinquish those limitations, slowly unfolding into a much more expansive version of who we can be.

We can start the work of healing from our traumas by getting curious about what is really happening in our life. We can start to ask questions like:

- *What inner conditions are holding me back in life?*

- *What limiting beliefs do I hold about who I am or what I'm capable of?*

- *What beliefs do I hold about the world that hinder me?*

- *What habits or behaviors hinder my full expression?*

Depending on what we uncover or what we feel will best serve our healing journey, we may decide to work with a professional to navigate the residual impacts of any traumatic experiences from our past. In any case, this is the work of healing: recognizing what is holding us back and committing ourselves to the journey of healing those things. Note that this is not about fixing our symptoms; it is about getting to the underlying beliefs, memories, or patterns that contribute to our surface issues (i.e. never committing to relationships, harboring low self-worth that hinders our professional success). When we treat symptoms only, we leave the real issue untouched.

Ultimately, we cannot change what has happened in our past, but we can decide what we will do from here on out. Just like forgiveness, this commitment to self-healing fuels freedom. Healing is available to all of us, even if it looks different from one person to the next. The particular healing journey we take and the modalities explored on it will be unique to our personal inclinations and needs.

There are various techniques and practices that can support trauma work. From one angle, we can explore practices of mindfulness, meditation, and breathwork to help increase our capacity to recognize what is holding us back, to sit compassionately and non-judgmentally with our struggles, and to work through these struggles. From another angle, we can explore psychological or physiological therapeutic techniques, such as neurofeedback, biofeedback, or cognitive-behavioral therapy. Various other forms of individual or group therapy can also be supportive. There is no right or wrong way to engage in self-healing; the best approach is the one that suits us in any given moment.

Practices for Forgiveness and Self-Healing

There are a variety of different practices we can consider to enhance our capacity for forgiveness and to fuel our self-healing journey. As noted, forgiveness grows from the seeds of strength, resilience, gratitude, compassion, goodwill, and generosity. Practices that focus on the cultivation of these qualities and virtues can help us open wider to forgiveness.

Furthermore, we can consider meditation practices that focus specifically on enhancing the process of forgiveness. These practices often include elements of the above-mentioned seeds that are required for forgiveness to flourish (i.e. compassion). Where self-forgiveness is required, consider the following practice.

1. Self-Forgiveness Meditation

Take a moment to settle into a comfortable seat, close your eyes or soften your gaze, and settle in through a minute or two of mindful breathing. Once you feel settled, call to mind a situation that would benefit from you widening your capacity for self-forgiveness. This could be an exchange or event that occurred during which you said or did something that felt out of alignment with your values.

Once you have recalled this particular situation, allow whatever associated emotions come up to be there – without resisting them and also without attaching to them. Allow the flow of emotions to come and go. If you notice words of self-judgment arising, soften these as you return to your direct experience of this moment.

Stay with these emotions for up to a minute and then ground your attention in your breath. Notice the rise and fall of your chest or belly as you breathe. Place a hand on your heart and repeat the following affirmations:

- *May I mindfully recognize when I act out of alignment with my values.*

- *May I release self-condemnation for things I have done in the past.*

- *May I acknowledge my faults and my struggles and forgive myself, committing to new ways of being going forward.*

- *May I release shame, acknowledge guilt, and commit to my personal growth.*

- *May I know that I am loved and that I am forgiven.*

As mentioned, forgiving ourselves may help to increase our ability to forgive others. We deepen our awareness of the fact that all humans make mistakes and that all humans act out of alignment with the virtues of compassion, respect, and goodwill from time to time. Forgiveness helps us to learn from these mistakes and to grow into a more aligned version of ourselves.

Forgiving ourselves is indeed a step towards self-healing. Additionally, we can use meditation to connect with our higher self and cultivate the wisdom that will best support our healing in any moment. Read through the following practice and consider it for yourself.

---

ayam™ TIP

ayam features two truly immersive meditations: Forgiveness and Self-Healing. I wholeheartedly recommend these practices for everyone.

---

2. Higher Self Meditation

Begin this meditation as usual by finding a comfortable place to sit, softening your gaze or closing your eyes, and taking a few mindful breaths. Feel into the surface beneath you for an extra sense of being supported.

Once you feel settled, call to mind a self-limiting thought or belief that is in need of transformation. As you call this thought to mind, keep a bit of distance between you and it. Notice it from the point of view of an observer. You might also notice what this limiting idea feels like in the body. Is there tightness associated with this thought? Is there contraction? Is there some other sensation?

After a few moments of observing this thought or belief, see if you can locate the voice of your higher self. What does it have to say about this self-limiting thought?

If you have difficulty connecting with your higher self, you might imagine the voice of another wise, benevolent being – plant, animal, human, or mythic being – entering into your awareness to offer words of support, transformation, and healing. This is an aspect of your higher self, even if it presents itself as something or someone else.

Continue to ask the questions:

- *What does my higher self (or another wise being) have to say about this self-limiting thought or belief?*

- *What words of support, transformation, or healing can be offered here?*

This practice may feel effortless on some days and difficult on others. Ensure that you practice this with patience, self-compassion, and care. Know that there is always a higher self inside of you that can offer you supportive, transformative, and healing words at any time.

Please note that this practice is not advised for those suffering from certain mental health conditions, such as schizophrenia. Consult with your healthcare provider before practicing if you suffer from any mental health disorder.

Journal Prompts

To enhance your awareness about where forgiveness may be needed and in what ways self-healing might be called for, take some time to sit with and write in response to the following questions.

1. What experiences or interactions from your past could use self-directed forgiveness?

2. What barriers do you have to forgiving yourself? What would your higher self say about these barriers?

3. Is there someone in your life that you can expand your capacity for forgiveness towards?

4. What do you think you need in order to enhance your ability to offer this person forgiveness?

5. What situation in your life needs your attention? What does it need or desire from you (i.e. compassion, patience, non-judgment, trust)?

6. What self-healing modalities or therapies speak to you the most?

I can forgive but I don't know how to forget

Over my lifetime, I have had the opportunity to work with three distinct lenses and contexts in supporting people to invite healing and forgiveness in their lives. The first is in the context of Life Coaching, where the focus has always been on getting people to focus on the future, and 'letting go' of the hurt that lay in the past. I noticed clients move forward very fast and yet something about them always gave me a sense of a certain degree of emptiness in their eyes, below all the enthusiasm, optimism and even drive. In my work with an international training and development organization, I was blessed to work with people in creating a "new future". I am truly grateful for that experience, where I had moments of wonderful learnings that I will forever cherish. That being said, I just could not shake off the feeling that I need more tools to support their transformation, allowing for more freedom. One day, a client said something to me that helped the penny drop into place. He approached me and said, *"I am committed to bringing transformation in my life, but I don't want to be a blind person seeking 4 eyes. I want to be free of the "trauma" of being blind or having been blind even when I get my sight back!"* I am sure I gave some wise answer to this 28-year old IT CEO and although I no longer remember what it was, his inquiry left me wondering: How might the "feeling whole" be integrated into the journey of healing and forgiveness?

The second lens came to me on my spiritual path, firstly while being trained as an energy healer and secondly, as a Buddhist monk. Both the doctrines - energetic-karmic ties and impermanence were very helpful for me to support the journey of my clients and I sensed that they were able to find deeper levels of healing and moving forward. And then one day, a fifty-two-year-old lady asked me the question, *"How can I go back to being the version I was before this trauma? It seems like not only my heart but my mind and my body have been broken."* I think for the first time in my life I realized how much the "physical" consequences of lack of forgiveness can have an impact on someone. I was inspired to explore how this might be healed!

In some ways, this journey found its own logical progression as my life led me to researching and working at the intersectionality of neuroscience, psychology, and biological medicine. This introduced me to the world of research around trauma, the work of pioneers like Dr. Gabor Maté, MD, and the amazing and mystical world of Bio-Neural therapy *(used in European Biological Medicine)* which, when combined with breathwork and ontological work by masterful practitioners like Dr Joy, MD, had the capacity to create tremendous spontaneous healing experiences for patients. Both in my research and search, I have not found something more powerful, and I genuinely feel blessed to have found a paradigm of healing that I could introduce to people who needed it most. And then I came across a client who sought a call with me to thank me for introducing them to this paradigm and she said, *"I can feel in every cell of my body that I am healing, all the memories and aches and pains that held me back are being released, it's like having a new birth – I am so grateful for this healing. I have forgiven and let go of the past. I do, however, have a question. How can I now work on forgetting?"*

I have forgiven but how do I forget? That is the question. I don't know the answer to that, I don't even know if it's possible or necessary for healing to occur. I just know that forgiving and forgetting are two distinct things, and one does not necessarily lead to the other. Some people may find it easy to forget, some may never forget. However, pain associated with the memories can be relieved. This is where the world of meditation is very helpful. As my mentor used to remind me, some pain is inevitable but suffering is always optional.

Final thought: Self-healing and forgiveness are two distinct journeys. They support each other and are highly correlated, but one does not automatically lead to the unfolding of the other. This has been my greatest realization in all my work in this field. Hence, in the ayam app, we have two distinct journeys. And while I am still making up my mind about it (the scientist in me is waiting on more data), when self-healing and forgiveness have both been completed, the natural arising of forgetting (in a wholesome way – not a trauma response) can actually become available. Or the memories lose the "charge", which is the true intent of forgetting anyway!

CHAPTER 12

Family, Friends, and Faith

Self-expression is the expression of who we are, which is made manifest through how we engage with the communities we are a part of. Aside from the workplace (which we will explore in a later chapter), there are three predominant communities with which we share a substantial bond: family, friends, and faith.

These communities are like three legs or pillars of a stool. For balance, all three are required. This does not mean that we only require these communities in our life in order to thrive, but it does suggest that they are foundational. Our workplace community plays its role, but it comes into our life much later, hence having less of a formational impact on who we truly are, in contrast to our relationships with friends, family, and faith.

It is important to note that there is no dogma in how these pillars manifest in our lives. For instance, our family does not have to be biological and our faith does not have to adhere to any particular religion or tradition. What matters is the quality of our relationship with each of these communities, which will be expressed in our own unique way.

We will begin our exploration with the first pillar – the community within which we all begin this human journey.

The First Pillar: Family

No matter what shape our family took as a child, we were all born into a family. Our family at the time of birth (and throughout our formative years) was our first experience of the world and of what it means to be in a community. It is also where we experienced our first sense of meaning. And we were, ultimately, shaped by those we had around us as an infant and as a growing child: by our parents or caregivers, elders, siblings, and the rest of our extended family.

Some might not have had both parents in the household growing up. Others might not have had siblings or elders. However, we all had a family, irrespective of the shape it took. And for better or worse, our first family created a template for nearly everything we would go on to experience in life. This is due to the defining effect of a family – it's an inherent way of shaping who we see ourselves to be, what beliefs we hold, what relationships mean for us, and how we express ourselves. Some of these defining ways of being are forthcoming and obvious to us; some are invisible, or unconscious.

For example, let's imagine we were born into a family with two loving parents who struggled to make ends meet. Let's also imagine that we were the fourth of five children and that there was always a struggle to get enough at the dinner table. These early childhood conditions could have shaped us in a variety of ways. However, for one child, this experience might have shaped strong competitive tendencies and a deep commitment to their career in order to avoid that experience again. For another child in the family, the sense of lacking abundance might have instilled inner beliefs based on fear and dependence, along with low self-worth. It is important to note that each child reacts differently to their circumstances.

As the example illustrates, how we respond and react at work, in our relationships, and in society at large is defined by what we learned from our family. Upheld virtues, prized ways of being, and traumas are just some of the ways we are conditioned. Trauma, which we explored in the last chapter, can be major or minor. For instance, being born into a family that prized education above play or faith-based participation above athletics could be enough to leave a defining mark on us. If certain interests or talents were left untended, denied, or punished, we are likely to hold conflicting and limiting views that do not serve the totality of who we really are.

In the same way, the virtues that were celebrated in our early family unit impact us through adulthood. For instance, if we were raised in a family that believed strongly in goodwill and the will to do good, this will undoubtedly have a shaping effect. Forgiveness, love, kindness, and any other virtue that was modeled would also have impacted us. In fact, all the ways in which we were nurtured would have helped to strengthen us.

For better or worse, shaping through our early childhood experiences is impossible to avoid. We cannot escape the basic process of conditioning.

However, it is the awareness we bring to it and what we do with that awareness that matters. We also cannot say that our upbringing was all trauma or all strengthening, and it wasn't all 'normal' or 'ordinary'. Our experience growing up was full of shaping moments, some that likely contradicted other moments, to create a very complex set of beliefs and behaviors.

And while the tendency might now be to dive into an analysis of our earliest years, the first step is simply to consider that your experience of life in many ways mirrors your first experience of family. This shows up in all sorts of ways, such as in how we relate to others, what goals we pursue, how much happiness we expect during life, and what we get out of life as a whole.

To increase our awareness of this impact, we can take a step back and notice what our relationship is to our nuclear family and also to our extended family, our friends, and society as a whole. How does our current experience of family (and of all other communities for that matter) reflect what we experienced earlier in life?

Then, we might consider how these formative years and the experience of family influences how we approach life as a whole and the building blocks of fulfillment. How do we approach meaning, fulfillment, engagement, and self-expression? How does our relationship to each of these building blocks mirror what we learned in childhood? Bringing this compassionate, non-judgmental awareness to these questions and our experience is the first step towards making meaningful changes for ourselves.

In doing this type of exploration, we might also ask ourselves: What emotions and experiences were allowed or even celebrated in my first family? And also, what emotions and experiences were not? It is important to remember that the intention of this work is not to lay blame but rather to increase self-knowledge so that we can more powerfully direct where we go from here.

Furthermore, it is worth noting that cultural characteristics can play a factor here. In other words, our early childhood experience of family is not based solely on the beliefs and personalities of those around us at that time. It also depends upon the cultural context they themselves were surrounded by.

For instance, some cultures are more rooted than others in the belief that families fight, but they stay together. On the other hand, some cultures prioritize loyalty before self-care and individuality. Yet others value individual freedom over everything else. As you explore your formative experiences, consider also how any cultural beliefs within your family and their community have influenced the beliefs and behaviors you embody today.

Ultimately, we are always part of a family, even if we are currently single or living alone. The family dynamic is always at play and it is always what we make it. If you are on your own or feel disconnected from a sense of 'family', consider that you are experiencing the solo aspect of being in a family and that 'family' might simply look different than how you expect it to look. For instance, your family might be defined by something other than biology.

In any case, no matter the shape of the family you are currently a part of, consider what the state of that family is at present. Does it provide a sense of support and meaning? How does it reflect what you learned all those years ago? And, where will you take your family from here?

The Second Pillar: Friends

After first experiencing the family we are born into, we broaden our sense of community by choosing our circle of friends. This is the first community we step into by choice rather than by default. As we move through life, we might notice that friendships provide us with different things (or that we ask for different things from our friends) but fundamentally, friendships offer a supportive, nurturing community within which to experience joy, growth, connection, and meaning.

As we look at the friendships we hold, we might consider how our early experience of family impacts these bonds. For instance, what part of ourselves are we expressing in our friendships? What is important for us in friendships and how does this mirror what we learned growing up? What do we offer to friends and what do we receive? Each one of us will answer these questions differently and we may find that they shift or evolve over time.

Asking these sorts of questions can help us to assess how much or how little our friendships contribute to our sense of well-being. This provides us with key insights that can help us to address any potential issues in our friendships that might be detracting from happiness. For instance, we might find that our friendships have become co-dependent and stagnant, holding us back from growth. Or, we might discover that our friendships are withdrawing more energy than they are replenishing, which might be leading us toward burnout.

Ultimately, our friendships should enrich our lives, not drain us. If we find that we are being drained or simply not receiving nourishment from our friendships, we need to start inquiring about what a healthy, nurturing friendship would look like for us. What is the balance between giving and receiving? What side of ourselves do we yearn to express in our friendships? What do we expect from our friends and what do they expect of us?

Expectations are not demands; they simply help us to know where our boundaries are. Every relationship needs its boundaries and we get to choose where we put the boundary in your friendships. Sometimes, we mistakenly believe that we should be completely open, completely forgiving, and completely selfless with others as if this were the highest virtue and a sign of true compassion. However, compassion is not complete if it does not include compassion for ourselves, which requires self-care. If a relationship is not serving us or is draining our energy, we need to consider what sort of boundary we could enact to truly take care of ourselves.

Remember that friendships come with agency – they are a choice. Where we might have had less of a say in our social network as children or teenagers, we have much more say over it now. We get to decide what works for us in friendship and what doesn't and ultimately, what we decide on should be of service to our overall well-being. This is not about judging certain friendships to be 'good' or 'bad', but it is indeed about asking the question: What do I need in my friendships to be nourished? What do I need less of?

The Third Pillar: Faith

Finally, we arrive at faith – the third fundamental pillar of community. Faith can be a source of dogma and conflict or it can be a source of strength, nurturance, longevity, and healing. Ultimately, our faith should offer a sense of unity and wholeness, and if it doesn't, we can serve ourselves and others by probing further.

But first, what is faith? Faith is what we believe in. It is the belief that we center ourselves around that helps us to understand who we are in this life experience. Faith is often associated with religion, but it does not have to be experienced this way. We can have faith in anything: religion, spirituality, certain values, science, nature, or something else entirely.

It does not matter what we have faith in because, beneath the content of our faith, the experience remains the same. For example, you and I might hold faith in different things, but the deep inner experience is more alike than different. For all of us, faith provides a sense of self. In fact, in our adult years, nothing has a more defining impact than our sense of faith. It helps us to answer the questions: Who am I? What do I fundamentally believe in?

Faith can undoubtedly be a nurturing, growth-enhancing experience. Once we have a sense of who we are and what we believe in, we can grow along that axis. For instance, if you have a fundamental faith in the Universe, that faith will deepen as you commit yourself to it. Likewise, if you have a deep faith in nature, this understanding will deepen and grow over time. We often think that our faith is set in stone and that we know all there is to know about it, but our experience and sense of self develop throughout our entire lifetime.

When we feel connected to a deep belief in something, it can provide us with longevity, inner strength, and healing. However, the difference between faith and dogma is a thin line. When we believe strongly in something, we can sometimes slip into self-righteousness or criticism of other people's faiths. Some of the greatest conflicts in the world have been based on faith and yet, so too have some of the most beautiful moments of togetherness, healing, and unity.

Thus, it is crucial to hold our faith with care and reverence for the faith that arises in other people. We can be deeply committed to our own faith while still respecting the faith of others. If you find this difficult, it can be helpful to detach from the content of the other person or group's faith and consider, "What does this bring to them?" Notice how your own faith nurtures you and consider how a different faith nurtures another. Again, the underlying experience of faith remains the same, even if it is placed somewhere else.

It is important to remember that your faith is your own; it does not have to make sense to anyone else. What is important is that your faith nurtures your sense of self and supports your overall well-being. Is it bringing you closer toward inner alignment and wholeness or further away from it? Does it yearn for room to grow, or does it need something else from you? As you bring curiosity to your experience of faith, you will uncover how it can further contribute to healing and wholeness.

Nurturing the Pillars

These three pillars – family, friends, and faith – are the mother spaces where you experience a sense of connection, meaning, and purpose. Well-being is not reliant upon these communities alone, but without them, we will find ourselves faltering. Each of these spaces provides immense value to our lives, and if we are willing to explore them with greater curiosity and commitment, we might discover where there is room for enrichment.

The key is not in judging where you currently are in terms of family, friends, or faith. Rather, can you simply notice where you stand right now? What is your relationship like with your family? What are your relationships like with friends? What is your relationship with faith? You can answer these questions by noticing how you express yourselves in each domain and considering how nourishing these elements of life are for you at present. Do they feel enriching or depleting? Do they feel balanced or imbalanced? Do they contribute to greater or less harmony?

When considering your self-expression in each domain, consider: Who am I with my family? With my friends? In my faith? What are the common denominators and where are there differences? Note the differences with curiosity, considering what there might be to learn from this insight. What does this tell you about yourself?

Consider also that, although family, friends, and faith are these beautiful spaces within which we find meaning, purpose, and connection, they can also become enclosed spaces, like ontological prisons, if we hold on too tightly or if we pass on and attribute all of our innermost inspiration to them. Faith and family most commonly, for instance, can either be nurturing spaces or they can keep our sense of self limited. The key is in finding a sense of deep connection to these communities while also ensuring we have space to breathe and room to grow and move.

If any of the above rings true for you, take a moment's pause to sit with this sense of resonance. Do any of these domains require more spaciousness? Is balance called for in your relationships to these spaces? What comes up for you?

To deepen joy and fulfillment in these domains, consider that it is typically not about forcing change or doing things differently. Often, what is required is a letting go. If there are certain attachments that do not serve you in any of these three spaces, consider what it would take for you to surrender these. Then, you can work to nurture these three pillars by coming back to the seeds of well-being: gratitude, goodwill, the will to do good, love, compassion, forgiveness, and self-healing.

So, which of these seeds of well-being is currently required in greater abundance by each of these three community spaces you find yourself in? In other words: What seeds can you plant in your family life? What seeds can you plant in your friendships? What seeds can you plant in the domain of faith? Take the time to sit with these questions in contemplation and make a commitment to some type of action that would nurture your well-being in each of these pillars.

📓 Journal Prompts

There were many questions offered to you in this chapter for contemplation. Some of those questions are repeated below along with further questions to prompt deeper investigation. Take your time to explore these questions, writing your answers down in a journal.

1. What virtues, emotions, and experiences **were** allowed and/or celebrated during your formative years?

2. What virtues, emotions, and experiences **were not** allowed and/or celebrated during your formative years?

3. How do your answers to the above questions shape the way you now express yourself:

   a. In your family? c. At work?

   b. With your friends? d. In society at large?

4. What does a healthy, nurturing friendship look like to you? Or, what do you desire and/or need from friendships?

5. What is the state of your current friendships? For example, how do you feel when you meet with your friends or after you meet with your friends?

6. How well does this state compare to what you desire and/or need out of friendships?

7. What does faith mean to you?

8. What do you have faith in?

9. Does your faith offer you a sense of growth, alignment, and healing or does it create conflict or unease in your life?

10. Is there anything you could let go of that would fuel healthy functioning in your family, friend, or faith communities?

11. What seeds can you spend more time planting and nurturing in your family community, in your friend community, and in your faith community?

The Popular Loner With a Big Family

One of my clients, Duli, is an archetype of the outgoing, extroverted professional. From the outside, his life seems to be full of friends, activities, and socializing. However, I have noticed that he always struggles with his weight. He has access to the best nutritional advice, eats really healthily and doctors don't find anything wrong in his tests, but he just can not seem to lose kilos. This, he has been telling me for years, is his number one worry.

One day, he sought time with me to have an urgent discussion. I accommodated him as soon as I could and he requested that we meet 'out of office' as he needed some air.

I drove to a nearby coffee lounge and just as he came in and we were done exchanging pleasantries, he said, *"I have something to share with you that has been keeping me up at night. Recently I was at a YPO meet, where the facilitator asked how many of us had at least one person or friend we can share anything with. I was one of the people who did not raise their hand. I don't have anyone in my life I can talk to without feeling judged."*

This experience had suddenly jolted him into a realization that he truly did not have a close friend in his life he could be vulnerable with. He was in a long-term relationship but did not feel comfortable sharing with his partner, as they had trust issues. He had a close-knit family but they lived overseas and he did not see them regularly. He had left home early for education in a boarding school and never developed the kind of closeness with his parents or siblings that would allow him to share his life with them.

He was sitting in front of me, under the weight of the realization that at the age of forty-five, he found himself very lonely. He had many other things to share. I heard him out, comforted him, and gently suggested that he could always reboot his approach to friendships. Adult friendships, albeit much harder to build, are certainly possible. I also shared with him that in my conversations with him, I was feeling like he had childhood trauma and he should see a therapist about it.

He took my advice and as he has worked through his childhood traumas, I have noticed he has become lighter and lighter at all levels. He has lost thirty-five pounds, slowed down in life, and is more present in conversation. He has found new relationships that are built around shared interests and hobbies, not professional networking. In general, he seems much happier.

I recently met him again and he shared that (I won't go into details here) he had a difficult experience with his parents in his early childhood that made him feel insecure, as a result of which, he never developed deep relationships. Now that he was working on these issues, he was, for the first time, beginning to feel safe around people and safe with himself. He closed by saying, *"If my parents only knew how much of my life would be shaped by something they thought was very small, they would have chosen differently."* and he would not have spent four decades running away from himself.

He says he now has people in his life who he not only knows well but who also truly care. And he is comfortable receiving that nurturing care. For the first time in his life, he feels loved and safe. At forty-nine, he says he is finally growing up and coming home to himself. I am so happy for him.

Family, Friends, and Faith are truly the determinants of how we will choose the die in which our experience of life is cast!

CHAPTER 13

Conscious Meaning-Making

Humans are wired for making meaning. We are genetically, cognitively, and evolutionarily programmed to do so. It is through meaning-making that we make sense of ourselves, others, relationships, and life at large. There is no way around meaning-making, nor should there be. The question, however, is: Are we aware of what meaning we are making?

Conscious meaning-making is about bringing awareness to this process of making sense of the world. First, it involves simply knowing that we are indeed making or reaffirming meaning as we move through life. Meaning is not just randomly or objectively happening; it is a subjective process that is shaped by everything we have experienced previous to this moment.

Second, conscious meaning-making is about being aware of the content of the meaning we make. What are we deducing about ourselves? About others? About life? We do not cultivate this awareness to judge ourselves as 'right' or 'wrong' for making a certain meaning; rather, we do so as a way of freeing ourselves from unconscious thought patterns that may be limiting us.

Each one of us makes meaning in our own way based on the predispositions we carried when we entered this world and on our experience as we moved through it. However, it is also important to note that meaning has evolved through the ages, just like our concept of happiness has.

Meaning-making Through the Ages

If we look back, for example, to the era of Plato, Socrates, and Aristotle, the making of meaning was perceived to be quite rational. For Aristotle, for instance, it was believed that you could understand something simply by considering its ultimate purpose or its end.[76] The ultimate purpose of life, he said, was happiness. As we look to Socrates, who famously said, "The unexamined life is not worth living," we discover an insistence to reflect on

---

76   https://www.psychologytoday.com/intl/blog/hide-and-seek/202101/aristotle-the-mean-ing-life

our beliefs, our values, and our motivations and to align ourselves with what we discover has real worth.[77] For Plato, the meaning of life was the pursuit of knowledge. He believed that we all have knowledge within us and that this knowledge is something we can rediscover.[78] He also believed that truth is not subjective but rather objective and that it can be known through reason used rightly.[79]

If we fast forward to the early 20th century, we come to Martin Heidegger who was a German philosopher and one of the main exponents of existentialism. Heidegger studied ontology, the branch of philosophy concerned with the nature of being, and through his work came to believe that being is independent of the mind. His views on meaning shifted throughout his life. In his earlier years, the meaning of life was really about how we can live an authentic life; one that is of our own choosing. Later, he believed that meaning rested in being 'guardians of the world'. The world, he believed, was something to hold in reverence, not something to be approached in a purely practical or intellectual manner.[80]

Jean-Paul Sartre, who also lived at the time of Heidegger, was another exponent of existentialism. His view was that life is inherently meaningless, but that through free choice we might give our life certain meaning. This was not, he is said to have noted, about being pessimistic. Rather than falling into despair, this lack of inherent meaning was a pathway for preparing ourselves for a genuine life and, like Heidegger, he believed in an authentic life.[81]

Another 20th-century philosopher who spoke of the purpose or meaning of life was Krishnamurti. He spoke of life ultimately having no beginning and no end and noted that life is what is right before our eyes. He said the significance of life is not something that can be either measured or discovered by the mind.[82]

These thoughts on the meaning of life are by no means exhaustive in their reflection of philosophers across time and culture who have had theories on what this whole experience of living is all about. The point is simply to note

---

77   https://iep.utm.edu/socrates/
78   https://blog.adioma.com/meaning-of-life-according-to-philosophy/
79   https://global.oup.com/us/companion.websites/9780190628703/sr/ch4/summary/
80   https://iep.utm.edu/mean-ear/
81   https://www.bu.edu/wcp/Papers/Cont/ContBhan.htm
82   https://jkrishnamurti.org/content/series-ii-chapter-28-purpose-life

that what we believe to be meaningful changes. Meaning is not fixed, given that humans across time have not been unified in their understanding of what this thing called meaning even is. Meaning, therefore, can be seen as what we make it.

The Ladder of Conclusion

Turning towards our internal mechanism of meaning-making, we can better understand how the process of meaning-making works by exploring the Ladder of Conclusion (also referred to as the Ladder of Inference).[83] Developed by organizational psychologist Chris Argyris, the Ladder of Conclusion is a model for understanding how our beliefs and actions are formed based on the data available to us, the meanings we interpret, and the assumptions and conclusions that we draw.

At the bottom of the ladder is all the data available to us (see diagram). We might say that this is 'simply life'. The raw data of our experience is what happens in our experience before we make any determinations about it, good or bad, right or wrong. Yet, have you ever observed that when data is presented, two people can interpret it completely differently? This is what happens as we climb the ladder.

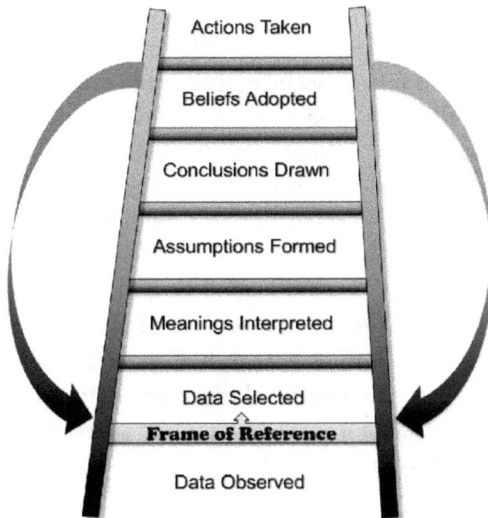

Actions Taken

Beliefs Adopted

Conclusions Drawn

Assumptions Formed

Meanings Interpreted

Data Selected

Frame of Reference

Data Observed

---

83   https://www.colleaga.org/tools/ladder-inference-avoiding-jumping-conclusions

The data we select is informed by previously adopted beliefs. We choose the data that suits what we have already concluded about the world, which leads us to form or reaffirm existing meaning. This leads to assumptions and conclusions, which confirm our pre-existing beliefs and direct our actions. Then, the cycle begins again.

When we are not conscious of this process, we tend to rush through the steps. We are left unaware that the way in which we are selecting and interpreting data is not governed by truth but rather by our subjective beliefs and experience. Thus, we reinforce what we think we know about ourselves, about others, and about life itself.

Let's look at an example to illustrate this:

> *Noah just heard back from a prospective employer with whom he had an interview. During the phone call, he learned that another candidate was given the position. However, the recruiter also mentioned that there was another vacancy Noah could apply for. For the original position, there was one vacancy and twelve people who were interviewed, but all Noah can now focus on is 1) the memory of the self-determined 'weird thing' he said during the interview and the brief silence that followed as the interviewer took notes, and 2) the fact that he didn't get the job. This is the 'data' he is selecting.*

> *He interpreted the interviewer's silent, note-taking pause as confirmation that he is too awkward for the social nature of the position (the meaning he interprets). His assumptions and conclusions follow suit, which reaffirms a long-standing belief that he is 'abnormal' or 'weird around people'. This belief fuels Noah's social anxiety, and the action he chooses to take is to not follow up on the other opportunity presented by the recruiter. He will apply for a job elsewhere.*

Chances are, we will not have to look too far to discover where this type of circular thinking occurs within us as well. Even if our underlying beliefs may be different from Noah's, the conclusions we've drawn about ourselves, others, and the world at large impact the actions we take and the way that we perceive the raw nature of our experience.

It is this very unconscious process of meaning-making that is responsible for habit formation and, in many ways, we need it to function. The psychological process reflected in the Ladder of Conclusion can help us to be discerning and to draw conclusions that are supportive of our well-being. For example, if we eat too much chocolate cake and pick up on the sensory experience of a stomach ache (data selected), we might draw the conclusion that too much cake is not good for us. Next time (or perhaps the time after that), we might remember this conclusion so that we do not need to 'relearn' through the experience of eating until our stomach hurts. As we know, in some cases, learning takes time.

With that said, much of the habits we form through this psychological process constrict our experience of reality. When left unexamined, we quickly jump from a narrowly-selected pool of data to a narrow conclusion and ensuing action. This is how biases, addictive processes, and narrow-mindedness form, which keep us entrapped in old stories and beliefs that do not serve a rich and expansive life.

The Impact of the Meaning We Make

The meaning we make, whether consciously or unconsciously, governs the course of our lives. It determines what we believe possible for ourselves, what we believe the world has to offer, what opportunities we seek out, and what actions we take. Though it is not always easy to see how the stories that play out in the mind impact the outer experience of life, the external is indeed a reflection of the internal.

For example, consider Noah once again. His meaning-making process directly impacted the conclusions he drew and subsequent action. Someone with a different set of underlying beliefs might have focused on two other data points: 1) that only one person out of twelve could be offered the position, and 2) that the recruiter was encouraging him to apply for another vacancy within the company. What type of conclusion and action do you think might come from selecting these data points as compared to the ones Noah selected?

The data we select and the way we process that data has a direct impact on our experience of life. Two people can encounter the same situation and walk away from it with a completely different take on what happened, what the meaning of the situation was, and where they take it from here. We tend to assume that our way of viewing life is the 'right' way because it is all that we know. We also tend to assume that we are seeing clearly when in fact, we are only seeing through our unique lens, and that can be very small or very wide, depending upon how mindful we are.

So, what determines the meaning we make? The invisible hand behind the Ladder of Conclusion is our sensory and emotional experience, such as our experience of joy, celebration, anger, and sadness. When we experience certain emotions alongside life events, they shape the way we perceive what happened and essentially become 'locked' in the meaning we make. Events, then, are reminders of emotions and emotions of events. These associations are what lead us to misinterpreting or narrowly interpreting things that happen in our lives. Again, this is not something unusual or wrong, but it is worth being mindful of because our emotions are not purveyors of absolute truth.

Ultimately, and to reiterate, the life we experience comes from the meaning we have made. For example, how we experience a rainy day depends on the way we view it. Is it an opportunity to rest and restore? Is it confirmation of how dreary life can be? Is it an opportunity for the soil to be nourished? Or is it something else? To experience a more fulfilling life, we need to address the way we are processing the details of it and this is possible through minding our meaning.

Minding Our Meaning

Minding our meaning is about bringing mindfulness to the way that we are interpreting the events of our life. It requires intentional but gentle action to witness and shape the psychological process that underpins our life experience. We can do this by actively cultivating two potentials:

1. Nurturing Virtues

First, we can remember that we have agency in the way that we think and act. When we remember that we play an active role in creating our reality, we can shift our focus to include the cultivation of virtues that nurture us. Virtues inspire us to make more wholesome meaning, which positively reinforces agency, nurturance, and growth.

As we nurture virtues such as gratitude, forgiveness, and compassion, we start to select data in different ways. For instance, if someone cuts us off on the drive to work, we will be less likely to jump to an assumption of wrongdoing. Instead, we might simply recognize, "That person is in a rush." Likewise, when something difficult happens to us, we will be better able to hold it in perspective, noting the blessings that are present alongside the challenge.

The virtues we cultivate also end up competing with any pre-existing biases we're unconsciously reliving or projecting. For instance, compassion will help us to soften the judgments we hold against a certain person or group of people, and naturally, our assumptions will shift. Someone has hurt us, we may be less likely to assume it's because that person is 'bad' and more likely because that person is suffering in some way. Not only is this a gift to another; it is a considerable gift to ourselves.

2. Cultivating an Attitude of Curiosity and Non-Judgment

Second, underlying mindfulness is an attitude of non-judgment. As we cultivate curiosity and non-judgment towards ourselves, others, and life as a whole, we naturally lessen our tendency to jump to conclusions. In fact, curiosity and quick conclusions are antithetical to one another. Curiosity requires that we seek more data and expand our understanding rather than falling into narrow, conditioned, quick filtering.

Cultivating an attitude of non-judgment is not about being unaffected by the meaning-making process. It does not require that we become incapable of drawing conclusions or taking appropriate action. Rather, it is about remaining perceptive and open-minded and about not becoming caught up in polarity. Too often we jump to conclusions that say, "I like this," or "I don't like this." "I agree," or "I disagree." "This is right," or "This is wrong." This tendency to latch onto a particular 'side' inhibits us from perceiving the complexity and nuance of life. It holds us back from seeing the bigger picture.

In Buddhist teachings, we see how meaning-making is one of the root causes of craving (in Pali – tanha; in Sanskrit – *trishna*) and of subsequent suffering (in Pali – *dukkha*; in Sanskrit – *dukh*). One way to avoid the suffering that meaning-making creates is by remaining open-minded and curious, and by refraining from latching onto good or bad, right or wrong, liked or disliked. This does not mean we never take action, but rather our actions end up coming from a place of wider perceiving.

At first, it might feel difficult or forced to cultivate certain virtues. Compassion, for instance, can be a challenge to harness in the face of hurt. Additionally, it might prove hard to refrain from jumping to conclusions of agreeance or disagreeance when in the midst of a debate or discussion. These ways of being are counter to many of the ways we were raised to be.

However, as you intentionally cultivate wholesome virtues and a mindset of curiosity, they will embed themselves within your nature. You will not have to 'think' about bringing them forth; they will be effortless. Eventually, they will become a natural part of your self-expression, leading to a richer life.

Living a Rich Life

How does conscious meaning-making add richness to life? Consider a bowl of homemade soup. If you draw a conclusion at first taste about whether you like or dislike the soup, you have determined what the experience of it is; there is nothing left to explore. It will either be simply dull or distasteful or it will be tasty. There is nothing wrong with tasty food of course, but is there more to discover here?

When you don't make your mind up so quickly about a bowl of soup (or anything else for that matter), you get to actually taste the full spectrum of flavors – the full experience. Rather than 'this is good' or 'this is bad', the experience becomes a multitude of nuanced tastes, textures, and even the temperature. The experience is richer and fuller.

The same is true for any other domain of life. Take yourself, for instance. How often do you fall into conditioned beliefs about who you are? You label ourselves as 'this or that', or 'not this or that'. However, what happens if you become more curious about your thoughts, feelings, actions, struggles, and tendencies? As you become more mindful, you start to realize that you are a dynamic and complex manifestation of life itself and not pinned down by what the mind might have to say about you. The same goes for how you experience other people and events in your life.

Finally, it is important to remember that there is no single, identifiable 'life' so to speak; there is only the meaning we make of it. When we realize that life isn't the narrow box we've come to see it as, we empower ourselves to create the life that is most authentic and meaningful to us. This is where true freedom lies.

Freedom is the greatest state we can experience as in a moment of true freedom, the possibilities are infinite. Freedom is not an external condition we must wait for; it is a way of moving through life that ultimately lives within. When we make a commitment to cultivating freedom of mind – freedom of our preconceptions, biases, and beliefs – the possibilities are endless. Anything is possible and everything we could ever hope to experience is available to us.

Journal Prompts

To get increasingly curious about the meaning you've made in your life and where there might be room for expansion, consider the following journal prompts.

1. Write out five beliefs that you hold about yourself, about others, or about life. Include both positive/uplifting and negative/limiting.

2. How does each of the five identified beliefs impact the relationship you have with yourself? How does each impact your relationships with others? How does each impact your relationship with the world?

3. How does each of the five identified beliefs shape the actions that you take in the world? Write down specific examples if you can recall any.

4. How would curiosity and non-judgment shift the negative or limiting beliefs that you hold along with the impact they have on your life?

5. What virtues would help you to shift the limiting beliefs you hold and the impact they have on your life?

What Are You Making It Mean?

At one stage in my life, I was training in a certain form of psychotherapy under a very senior and highly respected Psychologist based in Houston. I was really enjoying the process as it was a unique opportunity for me to focus on the 'process' of therapy rather than the content, which was markedly different from my previous training in leadership development.

One day in the class, we were having a mock therapy session, where the facilitator asked us to bring a real issue from our life to the practice. They suggested we pick something we were conflicted about. I picked something which at that time was a 'burning issue' for me. For reasons I can't go into here, I had recently decided to exit a long-standing business partnership on account of a difference of values. I was being pushed by a certain set of investors in the business to take legal action to protect my commercial interests. I am not a person given to engage in conflict; usually, I just choose to walk away. But this time it somehow didn't feel fair and I was truly conflicted about what to do. The issue was weighing me down both emotionally and physically.

As the session started, it very quickly reached a point where I was making the same argument that I did not want to create conflict – that it was against my values. The therapist heard it patiently and after diving a little deeper into the inquiry, asked me a question: *"Taking the legal route... what are you making it mean?"*

For a few moments, I was taken aback, and really thought about it. I realized that I was making the legal option mean, *'I was being greedy and vindictive'.* On sharing it with her, she asked me if that was my intention. I said no. She further asked me, "Do you realize you are making this meaning? The act in itself does not have this meaning by default." I realized that right away, and then she prodded further, "What are the other empowering meanings you could make?" After a while of introspection, I landed on 'setting boundaries' and 'advocating for self-interest'.

The moment I said that, it was like a ton of bricks lifted off my chest. As I felt unburdened of making a disempowering meaning, and choosing a meaning that set me free. And from that space of freedom, I completely lost interest in the legal option as well as the conflict related to it. And I was very happy with that choice.

Since that day, I have spent a lot of time examining the whole process of making meaning and, in my work with mindfulness, I have realized that 'conscious meaning-making' is a huge determinant of lasting happiness.

Anytime something in my life bothers me or I have difficulty letting go, I turn around and ask myself, *"What am I making this mean?"* Situations don't automatically change after that, but space within me to operate with peace and present-moment awareness certainly expands right away!

CHAPTER 14

Nurturing Purpose, Transcending Achievement, and Unfolding Actualization

Conscious meaning-making naturally leads us into an exploration of our purpose. Just as it is a natural human tendency to create and desire meaning, it is natural to long for purpose. What is our reason for being? What contribution can we uniquely make? The drive behind these questions is our longing for purpose and, like conscious meaning-making, purpose adds depth and richness to our lives.

Yet, discovering a sense of purpose is not always so straightforward since it means different things at various stages in our life. As we nurture our sense of purpose, we help it to naturally unfold and in that process, we shift from a longing for achievement-oriented purpose to a more natural, deeply embodied (or actualized) reason for being. Let's explore what this process may look like.

The Journey of Unfolding Purpose

To discover a sense of purpose, we need to consider that it is not something we 'find'. Often, the phrase 'find your purpose' feels like a tall order, understandably. Typically, we approach purpose as if it were hidden in the perfect job or only possible when we achieve a certain milestone. Shifting to a paradigm that sees purpose as something that evolves and unfolds is in greater alignment with what true purpose really is.

So what is purpose anyway? We can consider purpose to be our divine destiny or what we are meant to do while in this life experience. In chapter 6, we talked about how purpose is aligned with 'duty' but not in the common sense of the word. Our duty (or our dharma) is not a task or chore we *need* to complete; it is what we are innately destined or designed to do. Just as it is not a chore for the sun to provide Earth with light and warmth, our purpose is not an obligation.

The process of unfolding purpose takes time, and the journey is not a straight line. Chances are, we have all had a glimmer of purpose – perhaps a deep sense of flow or resonance while engaging in some kind of action. And yet, that glimmer often fades. We might feel it one day and not the next, which can leave us confused about what we're really here for.

Additionally, we can experience false starts or setbacks when exploring our purpose. A promising career might not turn out to be what we expected it to be, or something that once felt aligned might no longer feel resonant. The point to make here is not that these are necessarily signs we haven't found our purpose, but instead, they could be signs that our understanding of purpose needs to expand or evolve. Alternatively, these false starts, points of confusion, or setbacks might be an invitation to consider if we are doing what we think we 'should' be doing or are expected to do, or if we are indeed acting in alignment with a deeper wisdom or calling.

As the process of unfolding purpose evolves, our purpose shifts from a goal or objective-oriented pursuit to one that is more service-oriented. For example, someone might initially believe that their purpose is to write a book that will inspire others to overcome their fear of public speaking. While this is a worthy pursuit, is this the divine destiny of that individual? What is beneath the surface of this goal-oriented sense of purpose? What might be the bigger story they are destined to unfold?

True purpose is contextually and materially different from a goal or objective. Goals have a finish line whereas purpose is a direction or a way of moving. The process of unfolding helps to reveal deeper shades of purpose and every time that you materialize or actualize a goal, you come to realize there is more beneath the surface. As you follow these realizations to their source, you unfold a deeper, richer, more multidimensional sense of what you are here for.

So, if you have had glimmers of purpose, perhaps a sense of being deeply immersed in your work or connected to a higher cause, what does it take to unfold purpose? The journey proceeds in three basic stages: nurturing the seeds of purpose, transcending achievement, and unfolding actualization.

Stage 1: Nurturing the Seeds of Purpose

Firstly, we can consider that each one of us has seeds of purpose inside of us. These seeds are the small glimmers of insight we experience when we feel aligned with something greater than ourselves. Each one of us can feel alignment with a variety of causes, movements, or duties, but part of the work is discovering what we are uniquely placed on this Earth to contribute.

To nurture something requires an acknowledgment that this 'something' is not complete and that its current state is not a permanent reality. When we nurture a child, for instance, we know that our nurturance supports their ongoing development and personal evolution. When we nurture a friend, the same is true. We are also continually evolving and, for that reason, we all require nurturance.

Seeds, too, require nurturing. Take a moment to consider what a seed or seedling needs. Sunlight, water, and nutrients all help to create the conditions that are conducive to growth and development. They require not too much and not too little, and sometimes they also need protection from external elements, such as heavy wind or frost.

Our purpose for this life experience also requires nurturance. In fact, we can consider it to be just like a seed. We might then ask ourselves: What do we need more of in order to discover our purpose? What do we need less of or protection from to unfold our divine duty? The answers we discover will be different from moment to moment and will vary according to our personal needs. As an example, however, inputs like meditation or space for reflection can support us in nurturing our purpose. On the other hand, we may need protection from distractions that make knowing our purpose more challenging.

It is important to note that setbacks or challenges during the unfolding process can be viewed as opportunities for growth. For instance, a seedling can develop strength under tough conditions (such as high winds). We, too, can consider that everything that has us stop in our tracks or pulls us off course is an invitation to get curious and to inquire a little deeper. In the same way, our accomplishments can encourage us to dig deeper. Often, when we reach a goal, we are left with a sense that there is something larger beneath the surface.

To get a sense of how purpose unfolds, consider the following example:

Maria had long felt called to work with children who come from broken families and to be of service to that pursuit. This was what she believed her purpose to be, which came with the goal of setting up a non-profit organization. As she committed herself to this purpose, she eventually achieved that goal of establishing a non-profit and, at the same time, her sense of purpose was shifting.

After building the organization and working directly to support children with healthcare needs, Maria realized her time and energy might be better-used lobbying for change and getting resources to other people who were doing fieldwork. Now, her sense of purpose did not feel directly connected to the personal satisfaction she received from working directly with children. She enjoyed working with children, but her purpose felt larger than that.

Her expanding sense of purpose led her to ask deeper questions, such as: What kind of ecosystem is needed to support these children as they become teenagers and adults? What new communities, infrastructure, and technologies are needed to build a new system?

In the early part of Maria's career, purpose was wrapped up with daily gratification or recognition. Now, as she explored new roles and ways of being of service (i.e. as a mentor to others in the field), she realized that purpose was not about her or any emotional satisfaction she might receive. Her focus was now on where she could have the greatest impact, not on how her daily interactions made her feel. In fact, she realized her work could become more about the children even as she moved further away from working with them directly.

Stage 2: Transcending Achievement

Maria's story sheds light on the journey toward transcending achievement. This is possible as we nurture our sense of purpose – as we get curious about it and dedicate ourselves to exploring it, nurturing it, and protecting it. In this anecdote, we can see how our sense of purpose shifts from being more personal and achievement-focused to bring about the ultimate impact we can have. Often, we discover that our highest potential to positively impact or to be of service looks different than what we first imagined it to be.

This illustration of transcending achievement highlights what this might look like in a business context. In addition, we can consider that this journey is also applicable in the context of a monastic life, or a life in which spirituality takes center stage. In spiritual spaces, there is often the desire to 'achieve nirvana' or to 'reach enlightenment'. Although at first glance the longing may be harmless, on the subtle level, there is a clear sense that where I am now is not okay – that this moment is not enough.

Consider another example, which illustrates how one's sense of purpose evolves in a monastic setting:

Josef always believed there was more to life than meets the eye. He struggled throughout his teen years and early adulthood with anxiety and depression, which led him to leaving his modern life behind and becoming a monk. He spent four years at a Buddhist monastery, committed to his goal, and then-declared purpose of reaching enlightenment. He studied and practiced with drive and commitment and experienced moments of what he described as 'pure bliss'.

After four years, Josef felt that still, there must be more to life – that his purpose for being needed expansion. Something called him to look deeper into his original pull to become a monk. He uncovered that there existed then (and still four years after first pursuing monkhood) a great deal of fear due to global environmental issues. He also realized that for four years he had been running from the world.

Furthermore, Josef discovered that what he cared about and felt most committed to was in fact the environment. He began to question how he could be of greater service to the planet and felt a pull to help regenerate the Earth. This took many forms, such as learning how to farm organically and opening a sanctuary that wove his Buddhist knowledge and experience into his love and commitment to the earth. His sense of purpose was widening and deepening.

This example highlights a couple of things. First, it illustrates that no matter where we are or what kind of life we are pursuing, the achievement impulse can be found. It also shows us that transcendence does not require us to give up our life and, in fact, doing so might be more of a 'run from' than a 'run towards something greater'. This is not to make Josef's impulse to become a monk 'wrong'; his journey was what it needed to be in order for him to learn what he needed to learn.

The achievement impulse (in both the business aspect of life and the spiritual side of things) is entirely natural. However, it is worth getting curious about what rests beneath the surface. What if, for instance, we somehow learned that the thing we wanted to achieve would not come to manifest? Would we be content with where we are now? Or, would we feel that things aren't okay as they are?

In the previous chapter, we explored how craving leads to suffering. Craving a certain achievement or even making simple statements such as 'this is good' or 'this is bad' inhibit us from knowing our true purpose. There is nothing wrong with goal setting, but what is the energy underneath the pursuit of our goals? All in all, does craving and chasing a goal feel to be in alignment with what it means to live purposefully? These are questions worth getting curious about.

So how do we go about transcending achievement? As with most processes, the first step is awareness. We cannot willfully push ourselves beyond the pursuit of achievement but, through inquiry, we can explore what hidden urges or desires are beneath the surface of our seeking.

When you transcend achievement, you reach a state where you feel fulfilled by being a part of something larger than yourself – something that may not have started with you and that may not finish with you. It is not about what 'I' can do; it is about what larger movement I am playing my role within. For example, consider all the cells in a particular organ of your body – your heart for instance. It is not about what a single heart cell can do; it is about what all of them are able to do together.

As you get curious and zoom out from any narrow, personal goals you are working towards, you unfold a journey of higher purpose or meaning. This supports you in connecting dots that go beyond one's own lifetime. It is a feeling of liberation from achievement and a step into being of true service. Transcending achievement does not mean we stop taking action or working towards certain outcomes. However, we start doing so from a deeper, wiser, more embodied place within.

Stage 3: Unfolding Actualization

> *"Every living organism is fulfilled*
> *when it follows the right path for its own nature."*
> Marcus Aurelius

When we transcend achievement, we unfold actualization. Actualization is our natural state of being when we stop trying to figure things out and let 'what is' arise. As we explored in chapter 7, self-actualization includes maximizing our potential, contributing to the social system we are a part of, and recognizing our interconnectedness. It is about finding our place within the whole.

As a reminder, maximizing our potential is not about how much money I can earn, how high I can climb on this ladder, or what big projects I can check off my list. It is about maximizing our potential for being. For example: What is my maximum potential for living in alignment with my purpose? What is my maximum potential for *being* in a relationship with my higher self? What is my maximum potential social contribution? Indeed, we say 'my' maximum potential, but the benefactor of our potential is something greater than ourselves.

It is also helpful to consider that purpose is ingrained into who we are. We do not have to 'achieve' it as if it were something to possess; it is within us. It's not about what we need to do or what we want to do. Our purpose is our divine destiny – what we are meant to do. The question, rather, is about how we might live our purpose in the same way the sun lives its purpose. How do we achieve this degree of ease, synthesis, and integration as a human being?

To unfold actualization, you can focus on nurturing the seeds of purpose and examining your current relationship to achievement. It is important to note that we cannot push ourselves to transcend something and that the path to actualization does indeed go through achievement. Eventually, however, you come to realize that achievement has a constraining effect that does not serve your full expression. The intention is not to make achievement wrong, or to say 'you shouldn't worry about achievement.' Rather, the goal is to rise above it – to not be limited by it. We can certainly source our inspiration from our motivation to achieve while also looking at what lies beyond this achievement. Beyond the limitations of achievement is where we discover greater congruence with purpose.

Actualization will be a natural result of nurturance and this deep inquiry. To support this journey, get curious about where you say 'I will achieve this today' or 'I will make sure to accomplish that by the end of the year.' What is the impulse behind these statements? What if you were to consider that you do not need to achieve anything specific to live your purpose? What if you took a pause to consider that purpose is simply who you are? How does this realization shift the way you engage with your work?

As we self-actualize, striving dissipates. Again, this does not equate to giving up all of our responsibilities or ceasing to take any action at all. It also does not require us to give up modern life and live monastically. As noted, an achievement orientation can show up in both business life and spiritual life, in modern workplaces and spiritual spaces. Thus, transcending achievement and unfolding actualization is not about *what* we are doing; it is about *how* we are doing it.

Another result of unfolding actualization is the unveiling of flow. We might have experienced flow in short bursts previously (which might have been glimmers of our purpose), but as we step beyond the barrier of achievement orientation, we find that our actions occur intuitively, spontaneously, and without the stress that so often comes with accomplishment. There is less thinking about what we 'should' do or what we 'want' to do; there is just doing.

It might be difficult to imagine what it would be like to unfold a greater sense of purpose or to step into a flow state of being. However, we hold ourselves back by worrying too much about 'what it would be like'. Instead, we can simply start asking the deeper questions and getting curious about our experience to see what insights are ready to arise. Ultimately, it is possible for everyone to take this journey and as one does, it leads to a life that is much richer, deeper, and liberated than what we have experienced before.

In the next chapter, we will step into a deeper exploration of how to find flow. Where does it live? How do we access it? We will explore the directionality of time and examine the 'place' to anchor ourselves to live our greatest life possible.

📓 Pause for Reflection: Purpose, Achievement, and Actualization

Cultivating an attitude of curiosity is as important for conscious meaning-making as it is for unfolding our purpose. To expand your understanding of what purpose is or could look like, consider the following questions. Note that you do not need to arrive at a so-called 'perfect' answer and some questions might leave you with follow-up questions rather than answers. Simply see what arises (and follow any further questions to see where they lead), knowing that unfolding purpose is a journey, not a destination and that you are right where you need to be.

1. Of everything stated in this chapter, what rings true for you?

2. How would you currently define your purpose?

3. What limitations or challenges do you perceive in how you currently define your purpose?

4. How can you nurture your sense of purpose?

5. What does the pursuit of achievement offer you? How does the pursuit of achievement limit you?

6. If you gave up your goals, how would you spend your time? What work would you do? How would you express yourself as a unique, wonderous human being?

Purpose: *What you want vs. What wants you*

Curiosity about purpose has been a constant companion in my life as I have gone through different seasons. I have found expression for it in many different platforms, ranging from working in the non-profit space with my spiritual mentor to volunteering for a self-development organization. In my work as a mentor, I have had purpose conversations with a wide range of people, ranging from Presidents of countries and CEOs of large corporations to volunteer workers in the aftermath of a natural calamity. A form of synthesis my learning has brought me to has caused me to think of unfoldment of purpose as an ascending experience. I am sharing below my personal philosophy.

The first stage of unfoldment of purpose is what I like to call **"What I want to Contribute."** At this stage, many of us feel a desire to use our talent, time, and resources to contribute to others, and we derive a great sense of meaning and fulfillment from it. Our selection of where we choose to contribute is often linked to our preferences and passion, ranging from environmental causes to education. It's usually a deeply personal awakening. For example, I have a friend and colleague who is the CEO of a large pharmacy chain, and I have witnessed his personal awakening of service, where he is now making not only accessible medicine available to the financially underprivileged but also giving away thousands of filled prescriptions for free – *as a random act of kindness.* His family has always had the vision of serving the needy, which has been at the source of their business, but his own personal purpose of making a positive difference at the bottom of the pyramid has left his own unique stamp on how his business is run. The deep sense of purpose in his eyes when he talks about his initiatives is a great example of how your personal sense of purpose can shape your overall being.

Another example I have seen of this is with my friend and professional collaborator, Jim Lippens, founder of the World Happiness Congress, Europe. He has a personal vision of touching over ten million lives in his lifetime, with a message and tools for nurturing happiness. He is creating a series of projects and platforms to accomplish that. A two-minute conversation with him is enough to see how passionate he is about his vision and one could say that this is now the purpose of this life!

The next stage of purpose unfoldment is what I like to call **"What wants me."** This is a stage where people have an awakening to be part of and contribute to something larger than themselves. They may not be in charge or even in control of goals and outcomes, but they see their talent and resource as being of service within the larger goal of the project/institution. At this stage, personal preferences matter a lot less, and a desire to be of service matters a lot more. People tend to think of themselves as a custodian or trustee of the vision and purpose, and it does not, at this stage, matter whether they receive personal recognition for supporting the purpose or not. You will notice that at this point, people are contributing not only their resources but also a significant part of their lives. An example of this I have watched very closely is that of an entrepreneur who turned his life inside out in service of a mission of making holistic health and well-being accessible to people around the world. This was a vision he did not conceive of himself but crossed paths with, and realized he can make a big difference in fulfillment of it. Since then, he has mostly worked behind the scenes, craves no attention, rarely thinks about his personal benefit, and has no boundaries when it comes to helping other people in this space make a similar contribution. He simply says, *"I am doing this not because I want to, but rather because it needs to be done."*

In the first two stages, there is a common factor of the desire to see the fulfillment of their purpose. Usually, it reflects goals and objectives that people want to achieve. There is a selfless and understated, but present in the background expectation, that this is a purpose that they will see fulfilled in their life. And, to a lesser degree, be recognized for having contributed to it.

The third stage of purpose is what I like to call, ***"Being in service of what is meant to be."*** The defining feature of this stage is unfoldment of a purpose, which is not only larger than the individual but also one that is not limited by a 'personal vision' of fulfilling it. This is a stage where you are willing to be part of serving a purpose, with the full realization that you may not see it fulfilled in your lifetime and that when it is fulfilled eventually in the future, no one will remember you or your contribution. This unfoldment requires breaking through the 'veil' of personal lived experience and aligning to the impermanent nature of self and the eternal nature of life. I have found this level of consciousness most common amongst spiritual masters and institution builders. Some revolutionaries in history have also been an example of this, especially those whose names we do not know. When you talk to these people, you hear in their voice and vision the inevitability of manifestation of what they are contributing to and a humble realization of their relative insignificance in the grand scheme of things. As one of my mentors put it, *"I eat the fruits of the trees I have not planted, so why would I not sow the seeds for trees I know they will grow into, long after I am gone, bearing fruits sweeter still?"*

I could not have expressed any better, the sense of freedom and liberation that comes from letting go of seeing the purpose fulfilled in your lifetime!

CHAPTER 15
Living Your Greatest Life: Past, Present, and Future

As we unfold our purpose and begin to self-actualize, we start to find that our life feels more aligned. There is less attachment to our past and less worry about what the future might bring. Actualization supports us in expressing ourselves fully and authentically and stepping into the present moment, which is where we uncover a sense of flow.

In one sense, we know that we are always living in the present moment, and yet our day-to-day experiences can distract us from this knowledge. For example, we have all had the experience of being in a car or on a train, and the next thing we know, we've arrived at our destination. Where has our mind been all this time? Often, our drifting mind carries us into memories of the past or visions of an anticipated, feared, or desired future. In these moments, we escape from what is truly present. We are here, but we are not aware that we are.

In addition to exploring what is required for us to actualize, we can fuel our sense of alignment by becoming more conscious of where we are spending our time. Are we reliving the past? Are we overly focused on the future? Or are we present for this moment as it unfolds?

By recognizing where within the directionality of time we are focused and by recalling our capacity to choose how we live in this moment, our greatest life becomes possible. Let's explore how each of these three time-based orientations impact our experience of this life.

> *"To live in the present moment is a miracle. The miracle is not to walk on water. The miracle is to walk on the green earth in the present moment, to appreciate the peace and beauty that are available now."*
> Thich Nhat Hanh

Making Peace with the Past

We all know what it is like to live in the past. Memories, both conscious and unconscious, shape the way that we engage with ourselves, with others, and with life as a whole. Conscious memories are those that we can mentally recall and unconscious memories are those that silently or energetically impact our lives without our full awareness.

None of us can escape from the fact that we have a past. No matter how much meditation we practice or how many self-help books we read, we will still have our past. What changes is not the content of our past but the charge of it. What shifts is how we *relate* to our past.

Making peace with our past is about taking the steps required to not be constrained by whatever came in moments prior to this one. This is not about denying, pushing away, or minimizing the imprint of past experiences. Rather, it is about acknowledging the shaping effect our past has had, recognizing how it impacts us today, and deciding where we want to go from here.

In chapter 11, we focused on forgiveness and self-healing, the entangled pair that supports us in releasing the past. We spoke of the importance of acceptance, which is not about liking or condoning anything that occurred in our earlier years but is more about refraining from arguing with reality and acknowledging that whatever happened cannot be erased. The past is not changeable but what we do with it and how we relate to it is indeed within our control.

We often think about the various ways that our past constrains us. For instance, we might recall how our parents never supported or celebrated our artistic creativity. Perhaps they only celebrated our academic achievements. This, we might reason, is why we struggle to find play and joy in life and, perhaps, why we now struggle to support our children in this way. This assessment may contain some accuracy, but the more important questions are:

- *What do we do with this knowledge?*

- *Where is forgiveness, wisdom, or deeper understanding required?*

- *What lessons have we learned from our upbringing?*

- *What has this experience revealed about where we have room to grow?*

- *What has this experience shown us about our untapped potential?*

As we compassionately and curiously investigate how the past plays into our future and nurture seeds such as forgiveness, self-healing, and gratitude, we lessen the charge or unconscious reactions associated with these memories. We also discover that we do not need to be held captive by our past; it does not need to limit us any longer. Note that, for many, it is recommended to explore one's past with a trained mental health professional.

It is also helpful to acknowledge that there may be some resistance to looking at our past. A whole host of difficult feelings can arise when we do: feelings such as shame, blame, anger, and grief. This is why support is beneficial, particularly where there is much trauma or a significant traumatic event in one's past. Self-compassion is also crucial for this process of self-healing.

Exploring our past, however, need not only be about lifting our hurts and traumas into consciousness. We can also honor what has strengthened us. What positive qualities have we developed throughout our life? What accomplishments have these qualities led to? Our past can certainly feel limiting, but it can also be the source of strength, courage, resilience, and other nourishing traits. We can choose to celebrate and to give gratitude for all the inner virtues that have uplifted and supported us along our way, that have supported our unfolding.

When we look at the memories we hold of our past, it is also worth noting that we don't always remember past experiences as they happened. Often, we recall the way we processed or interpreted those events after the fact. Now, we might be able to interpret them in a new or expanded way and so we can hold our memories with a sense of curiosity and openness, realizing that much of what we think we 'know' about the past is our story of it.

It is also important to note that making peace with the past is not a linear process. In one moment, we can experience immense gratitude, understanding, and insight, and in another moment, we might be swept away by limiting, conditioned responses to life. This is entirely natural as healing does not take a straight upward trajectory. Be patient, curious, and compassionate as you delve into your own healing journey.

Despite the fact that making peace with our past does not occur linearly, we find that over time the 'ups' surpass the 'downs'. And as the process evolves, we find that our understanding of ourselves and life itself are expanding. Over time, the charge of the past dissipates and we unlock our potential to choose where we go from here.

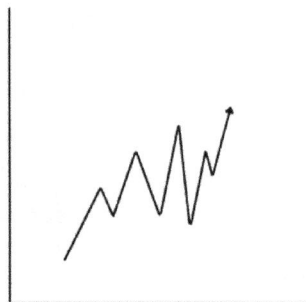

So ultimately, we all have a past and we always will. Everything we experience now, here in the present, will become the past sooner than we realize it. The question is: What might we do with it?

Framing Our Future

On the other side of time is the future. Unlike the past, we cannot remember the future as it has not happened yet. If we could remember it, we would be living from it. Yet while we cannot live in the future, our sense of it or hopes for it shape the actions we take today. Just as we do not drive a car solely by looking through the rearview mirror, we can also use forward-focus to consciously craft our reality.

This is why many self-help books focus on the future and on cultivating positive images or thoughts about the future to shape our reality. While this focus may be appealing to many, it can take us away from what is here right now and from realizing the freedom in this present moment. Furthermore, focus on the future can be used to escape or bypass the challenges we are currently experiencing. This might be tempting, but it will not help us to genuinely work through the root causes of our challenges.

Instead, we can see the future as a frame – a frame that is defined by our purpose. It provides a sense of direction, but it does not attempt to know what is to come. A frame does not force a certain outcome; it simply holds whatever comes into it. In this way, the future can be thought of as the possibility of actualizing our purpose while we remain connected to where we are now.

Furthermore, our purpose provides cadence and a direction for the future. As our purpose unfolds, it helps us to act in alignment with the greater narrative we are serving. When we understand our sense of purpose, it acts as a lighthouse to illuminate the way forward. It has an intangible quality to it and is not defined by anything specific, such as a career, milestone, or achievement. Careers, milestones, and achievements still come, but they are not the focus of our efforts. The focus is our purpose, whatever shape that takes, which is our guiding light.

It is worth noting that, often, the frame we hold for the future is dictated by our past experiences. For example, we might limit our vision for the future based on memories of prior challenges. As we draw mindful awareness to our dreams for the future, it is worth considering if we are constraining what we believe is possible based on pre-existing ideas, beliefs, and experiences. Awareness is the first step towards creating a future that is unencumbered by our past.

To frame our future, we can become curious about the non-specifics of our vision. We might ask questions such as:

- *What are the guiding principles of my life?*

- *What is the larger story I am here to serve?*

- *How might I surrender any worry or concern about the future?*

- *Can I release assumptions about the specific shape my purpose takes?*

- *Can I remain open to the mysterious unfolding of my purpose?*

- *What would I create or express if I were unencumbered by my past?*

These sorts of questions help us to understand the frame (or purpose) that surrounds our unfolding life. They also help to keep the space within that frame open and broad so that the future can unfold itself in accordance with its own wisdom rather than through the force of our human will. These questions can also help us to set the past aside so that we can usher in new life, breath by breath, moment by moment. As we relinquish our attachment to the future and limitations imposed by the past, we sink back into the place we truly reside – the here and now.

Finding Flow in the Present

"You must live in the present, launch yourself on every wave, find your eternity in each moment."
Henry David Thoreau

As we ground ourselves in the present moment time and time again, we unlock our inherent capacity for flow. Flow is a state of being in deep alignment with what is. Within this state, we find the freedom to choose, not out of fear nor out of conditioning but out of alignment with purpose and consciously-crafted meaning. When in flow, we may be aware of the past and future, but we are rooted and alive within the present. This is how we unlock our greatest life possible – by living in this flow and in alignment with what is.

When we live in the present, our life is not defined by achievements. We are not concerned with doing this or that; we simply do what we are called to do in the given moment. Our greatest life is defined when we experience a sense of freedom that 'life is'. There is nowhere to go, nothing to change, and nothing to fix. There is also no one we need to be. We simply 'are', and life simply is what it is. It is the freedom to choose in the moment that creates flow.

In this state of flow, our pursuit of peak performance expands. We will still achieve things, but our focus will not be so singular. Rather, in flow, we become driven by a whole-life sense of performance and a desire to be fully alive and self-expressed.

To align with the present moment and to sink into a stream of flow, we can sit with questions such as:

- *What is this moment asking of me?*

- *How might my purpose manifest in this moment?*

- *How can I be of service here and now?*

- *How can I live out my highest potential now?*

- *Rather than what I 'should' do, what am I called to do here and now?*

- *In this moment, what action would be congruent with my sense of meaning and purpose?*

These questions are not always so easy to answer, but that is okay. You can let them simmer, using them as fuel for your personal journey toward actualization. Sometimes, it is the questions that are more important than the answers as the right questions can be doorways into infinite possibilities. As Rainer Maria Rilke writes:

> *"... be patient toward all that is unsolved in your heart and to try to love the questions themselves like locked rooms and like books that are written in a very foreign tongue. Do not now seek the answers, which cannot be given you because you would not be able to live them. And the point is, to live everything. Live the questions now. Perhaps you will then gradually, without noticing it, live along some distant day into the answer."*

It can also be helpful to note that when we enter into a flow state – when we enter into pure presence – it is not that time stops ticking. The present moment is, after all, unfolding. However, what does happen when we enter into flow is that we become aware of the infinite nature of time and the expansion of the present moment. The future is not 'there' and the past is not 'there'. Our perception of the past, present, and future exist on one continuum, which is the ever-unfolding Now.

We can experience flow in any realm of life. Some people, for instance, experience flow in the kitchen or while painting. Others experience it while writing or playing with their children. In these moments when flow is present, there is complete congruence with purpose, which brings deep inner peace. This is not a restful peace but a peace of full dynamic actualization. As our journey unfolds, we experience flow in more and more realms of life. We realize that we can serve our purpose and create conscious meaning in many different ways – at home, at work, and in all moments in between.

When we are in a state of flow, our lives become the meditation. In these moments, we find ourselves not where we once were and not where we will be in the future. We are fully immersed in the present moment and fully embodying whatever the moment asks of us. If we are painting, we are painting with complete, dynamic presence. If we are writing our first book, we are doing so with full immersion. We do not worry about what our actions might bring; we simply trust that this is where we need to be.

Being in a state of flow also guides us to recognize the impermanence of all things. Everything we experience only lasts for a period of time. This recognition should not make us detached from life. It does not mean that nothing matters or that our experience is nothing. Rather, we can hold this recognition of impermanence as a source of inspiration and a reminder of our freedom to choose in *this* moment.

Since everything is transient, can we fully embrace that this moment is everything that we have? Can we hold the duality of the feeling that life is everything and nothing? Can we sink into the awareness that, quite simply, 'I am' and that my 'I am' is always evolving? And, given that we are always evolving, what will we choose now to evolve to our fullest potential? These are more questions we might sit with.

So, while memories of the past or visions of the future might pull on us, we can sink back into what is here and now. Work on healing and letting go of your past. Hold your sense of purpose as a signpost or a frame for your future. But ultimately, ground yourself in this present moment. Our life is what we make of it now and when we fully recognize and harness this power, our greatest life unfolds.

Pause for Reflection

In addition to contemplating the questions in the above sections, you can further unveil your greatest life by holding close the truth of your impermanence. Consider, for instance, that everyone who passes today had a plan for today; we simply never know when our time will come. With this in mind, we can ask ourselves:

- *What do I want to do with today?*

- *How can I live in congruence with my purpose today?*

- *If I knew I would die tomorrow, how much of my schedule would I change?*

Sit with the above questions first before exploring more nuance in the last:

- *If I knew I would die in a month, how would my schedule for this last month change?*

- *If I knew I would die in a year, how would my schedule for this last year change?*

These questions need not be somber. Rather, they can help us to become more aware of the truth that we never know how long we have and that the present moment is truly the only thing guaranteed. So, how will you bring more purpose and meaning into what you *do* have? How will you make peace with your past and frame your future so that you may experience your greatest life in this moment? Always remember that your greatest life is not behind you and it is not before you: it's potential lives right here in this present moment, and it is yours to harness.

I Remember the Future

Once on a flight from Thailand to Frankfurt, I sat next to the abbot of a local monastery. In the past, I had lived as a Buddhist monk so I automatically had a feeling of deep respect and deference for him. I helped him stow his luggage and settle in for a long flight.

I was keen to start up a conversation with him. After all, it's not every day you get a chance to sit next to a senior monk and have a casual conversation with him. Soon, the meal service started and we began a polite conversation. *"Bhante, I am honored to sit next to you,"* I started. The monk immediately understood that I was a Buddhist or a practitioner, well versed in how to address a monk with respect. He asked where I was from and I shared my journey with him. He was very curious about what was next for me. I was very intrigued. We continued to talk and I found myself thinking aloud about my future plans. Somehow, the conversation trended toward my past monastic experience and, unexpectedly, the monk was almost disinterested and brought me back to talking about my future.

After a little while, I gently asked him where he was going and received an eloquent answer about his vision of creating some new monasteries in Latin America. When I asked him how he started his journey as a monk, he smiled at me and simply said he wanted to serve the dharma now where it's most needed. I prodded a little more and he responded, *"Dear friend, I don't remember the past. I remember only the future, which is where my duty lies."*

Over the years, this phrase has grown on me. I have learned the tremendous value of being liberated from the constraint that the past imposes on our view of the future, and how empowering it is to create a future from the space of possibility, where anything and everything is possible. And the only boundary is your imagination and vision.

CHAPTER 16

Creating a **WOW** Workplace

We each live just one life, even if our one life is split into various 'facets' or 'roles'. Part of this one life is what we do professionally – the time and energy we spend at the workplace. If we have worked in numerous departments or companies throughout our lives, we know that there are all sorts of company cultures. From the dysfunctional to the exceptional and all in-between, each workplace is unique, for better or worse.

With working from home becoming the new normal post-Covid, the disappearance of physical boundaries between work and other areas of life has also been a huge disruption. When coupled with the digital devices we carry, our work literally follows us everywhere and at all hours. So, in some ways, the workplace has become a *mindplace* or *mindspace* where we are connected to work. In this new paradigm, the quality of work environment and engagement has become an even greater predictor of quality of life with respect to other facets and areas of our overall life.

Inbetween the extremes, there are a lot of 'good' workplaces. But what makes a workplace 'great'? What gives it that WOW factor that inspires employees and leads effortlessly to high productivity, creativity, and leadership? There are three key factors to consider to cultivate a workplace that goes above and beyond: engagement, positive emotions, and corporate mission.

Fostering Employee Engagement

The first factor or characteristic of a WOW workplace is employee engagement. To create an exceptional work environment, employees should always be fully engaged (and if not, issues should be addressed mindfully). At first glance, we might take that to mean that the employee should simply be fully involved in the work that they are doing for the company. However, full engagement requires more than that.

To be fully engaged, all parts (or levels/dimensions) of oneself must be engaged. A fully engaged employee is therefore not only fully present and involved in their role at the workplace, but they must also be participating fully in their life beyond work, and the dynamic they experience when engaged in work supports it. This is because it is very hard to be an exceptional, tuned-in employee if another aspect of our life is not thriving or at least being cared for. The person who makes themself coffee at 6 am and shares breakfast with their children is the same person who manages high-risk decisions and makes presentations at the workplace. The two are not separate, which is the one life hypothesis: who we are in one area of life ripples into who we are in another area, or more rigorously speaking, all other areas of our lives.

While harmony between our parts is the goal, this is not always the case. If one part of who we are is at odds with another part, care, and attention need to be brought to this inner division. To better understand this, consider the following example:

> Lena is the top sales manager for a multi-million dollar company. She loves what she does (and she's great at it) and anyone who knows her would call her a high achiever. She gives the company "all she's got." Outside of workplace concerns, Lena has some of her own. She's been starting to have signs of cardiac problems and, as a result, is feeling anxious and starting to question how she's been living her life. She wants to be healthy and well for her children and she wants to feel more fully engaged in their lives. Due to the high demands of her position, her husband has been taking care of most things at home, which has also put a strain on their relationship.

Lena's story exemplifies how different parts of ourselves can be at odds. Here, we see at least three parts: the part of Lena that loves her work and wants to succeed; the part of Lena that requires self-care; and the part of Lena that wants to be more fully engaged with her family.

In a WOW workplace, Lena would feel safe and comfortable to acknowledge all of her parts. She would be supported in expressing her needs, experiencing positive, nurturing emotions, and in receiving help and support as needed. Lena would not have to deny the rest of her life in order to succeed at what she does. She would have a supportive community to share her whole self with and mentors to nurture, guide, and support her. When nurtured in the workplace, Lena could then go back and nurture the other parts of herself and her life as a whole.

Full engagement also requires an individual to be aligned with their job content. We each have unique interests, talents, and skills, and to be fully engaged at work we must be able to express these personal inclinations. In a WOW workplace, employees are a good fit for their position and where there is incongruency, employee and employer feel safe to explore what alternatives might suit the needs of both parties.

Ultimately, employee engagement occurs when the workplace supports the totality of who the individual is. It celebrates the unique gifts, insight, and potential of each employee and seeks to support them in integrating all the various facets of who they are. In an exceptional company, it is acknowledged that each employee's life extends beyond the walls of the workplace. We know intuitively that someone who is stressed, frustrated, angry, or resentful – even if outside of work – will not be sustainably productive at work. Equally, a worried father or mother, a disenchanted spouse, or an angry global citizen typically does not make the best workmate – or at the very least, they will struggle to bring the best version of themselves to work.

Therefore, for the well-being of the individual and the collective, the WOW workplace focuses not just on what it needs to thrive but also on how it can help *its employees* to live a WOW life. Consider: What could that look like? What might that make possible? What would a society or culture look like if WOW workplaces were the norm?

As we begin to engage with these questions and work on fostering fully engaged employees, we encounter the potential to help our employees cultivate positive emotions, which is the second feature of a WOW workplace.

Nurturing Positive Emotions

The WOW workplace not only supports full employee engagement but also helps individuals to cultivate positive emotions. Positive emotions include things like joy, peace, calm, love, and gratitude. While we cannot force positive emotions onto people, we can create an environment that helps employees to cultivate them for themselves. This is done by creating a more mindful workplace – a place that embodies qualities such as compassion, non-judgment, care, and curiosity.

For example, consider one of the most common processes that occurs in any organization: communication. When we bring mindfulness and its related qualities to communication (i.e. compassion, non-judgment), we create an environment in which employees feel safe to be vulnerable and express themselves. It fosters openness, honesty, and transparency and, on the flip side, reduces mistrust, secrecy, and resentment.

By creating a foundation of mindfulness, we help to bring out the best in our employees. We help them to feel good about what they are doing and we also create space for support and care when things aren't going so well. To this point, nurturing positive emotions is not about denying more difficult emotions. When difficult emotions or conflict arises, it is addressed directly – with care, compassion, and curiosity. This helps individuals within the organization to move through any difficulties or negativity so that positive feelings can then flourish naturally.

Let's consider Lena's story once again:

Lena's heart issues come to her as "a wake-up call." She realizes something needs to change about how she is working, but at the same time, she fears having a conversation with her boss about this issue. What if her boss thinks she is no longer up for the task? What if she ends up losing her job? Lena spirals into further anxiety and is unsure about what to do. She is also highly attached to her work and so there is resistance toward making changes.

In a mindful workplace, a culture will have been created that fosters care, transparency, authenticity, and vulnerability. Lena would feel safe to share her concerns with her managers or, if the anxiety were still present at the start of the much-needed conversation, they would be quickly put at ease. Lena's managers would not just preach mindfulness, care, and compassion. They would *embody* it.

It would be clear to Lena that her whole self was welcome here and that her self-care was just as important as the care and devotion she gives to the company. The company would support Lena in cultivating the positive emotions she requires to thrive – not just at work but also in the rest of her life. This would be made clear in everything from communication and hiring to performance appraisal and opportunities for learning & development.

In addition to nurturing positive emotions when difficulties arise, managers can also actively support the cultivation of positive emotions more generally speaking. Many workplaces focus almost exclusively on deadlines, goals, growth, and ultimately, the bottom line. While the bottom line is important for the longevity and well-being of the company, so too is employee morale. One study, for instance, found that happy workers were 13% more productive than their counterparts.[84] Another study found that 66% of employees would likely leave their job if they did not feel appreciated.[85]

There are numerous ways to cultivate positive emotions in the workplace. The primary way is to have upper management work on embodying mindfulness since positive emotions naturally arise from there. Cultivating and embodying mindfulness is explored later in this chapter, but a few simple actions and considerations that management can take include:

- Expressing gratitude for employees

- Shifting the focus from 'tasks and goals' to 'accomplishments and contributions'

- Honoring the multi-dimensionality of employees (i.e. their need to rest)

- Encouraging self-care (i.e. creating a meditation room, offering well-being workshops)

Both engagement and positive emotion contribute to the natural arising of meaning and purpose. However, there is also a third factor that helps a workplace to meet its full potential: that is, corporate mission.

Inspiring Through the Corporate Mission

The final key to crafting an exceptional workplace comes from inspiring employees through the corporate mission. Employees want to feel like they are a part of something and the company mission (and vision) helps them to know what they are contributing to. Sometimes, employees are highly

---

84   https://www.forbes.com/sites/forbesagencycouncil/2021/04/16/if-you-want-to-be-more-productive-at-work-get-happy/?sh=6573176f7be2
85   https://www.forbes.com/sites/victorlipman/2017/04/15/66-of-employ-ees-would-quit-if-they-feel-unappreciated/?sh=6974aac96897

aligned with and engaged in the content of their job but not with the corporate mission. Sometimes, the opposite is true. Consider the following example:

> Taylor works in customer relations for a major food importer. He loves engaging with and supporting people, so he thoroughly enjoys the nature of his job. Since he's quick, attentive, and organized, he is good at what he does. However, Taylor has been starting to feel out of alignment with the company's mission. He cares a lot about sustainability and he knows that much of what the company imports does not meet sustainability best practices or fair trade standards. As time progresses, Taylor feels more and more disenchanted with his workplace and he knows that others in the company feel the same. In fact, many of them discuss it quietly amongst themselves and some are looking for other jobs.

This is an example of an employee who is engaged with the content of his job but not in alignment with the corporate mission. Furthermore, we learned that Taylor is not the only one – many employees are questioning the mission and practices of the business.

An exceptional company would take the time to get to know the values of its employees. What matters to them? What will keep them engaged? While upper management is ultimately the one responsible for creating the mission and vision and does not need to change its direction for employees, the key mindfulness principle of curiosity would serve the company well here. They might start to ask themselves: Is there an opportunity to commit to something really positive here? In what way could the company learn and grow?

When the situation is reversed, an employee might find themselves in full alignment with the corporate mission. However, they may not be well-suited for or enjoy their specific job. If their skills and interests could find better expression in another position, a mindful workplace would create space for a caring conversation around this matter to take place because, ultimately, ensuring that employees are a good fit for their position benefits both them and the organization as a whole.

So as employees, it's not enough to simply like what we're doing or to simply like what the company is doing – we need both. What are we a part of? What are we contributing to? These questions help to further enhance a sense of meaning and purpose and when explored with upper management, these queries can fuel organizational growth as well.

The Unlimited Potential of the WOW Workplace

These are the three legs of a WOW workplace: full engagement, positive emotions, and alignment with the corporate mission. What becomes possible when all three of these are present? A new dynamic full of potential.

When a workplace checks off these three boxes, the whole network or workplace ecosystem comes online – fully engaged, positive, inspired, and aligned. What this leads to is unpredictable, though typically we see performance, creativity, commitment, and ownership all increasing alongside the cultivation of these three features. The impact is both quantitative and qualitative.

When employees are fully engaged and have a solid foundation of positive emotion and inspiration, micromanaging is not necessary; work becomes self-driven. Each individual takes responsibility and direction, leading to increased flow and effortlessness of corporate activities. No longer do we need to push or force or control. The company's destiny is driven by all the wonderful, skilled people who comprise it.

Creating a WOW workplace is something like tending a garden. You plant the seeds and provide the nurturance each being needs to blossom, but you do not have to force the plant to grow. That force comes from an innate intelligence all its own. Think about the difference between a garden left without much care and one that is well-tended. As you envision the potential of that second garden, you tap into the energy of what may be possible in a WOW workplace.

Leading With Mindfulness

What is the common denominator between these three legs? Mindfulness. Mindfulness underlies them all and supports us in cultivating them. So, to create a WOW workplace we can begin by focusing on bringing forth all those qualities that are linked to mindfulness – qualities like compassion, gratitude, transparency, honesty, and curiosity.

We talked a bit already about how this can be brought forth. Communication, for instance, is one of the most common processes within a workplace. It flows like a web between all members within an organization and between internal and external parties (i.e. out to customers and suppliers). However, mindfulness can also be brought to other core processes, such as hiring and firing, performance appraisal, and learning and development. Examples include:

- Cultivating kindness and compassion before letting an employee go or conducting a performance review

- Extending gratitude to employees and customers

- Listening to customer complaints with curiosity and non-judgment

- Providing employees with opportunities for personal growth (i.e. mental health talks, meditation classes, stress reduction training)

- Being mindful of biases or judgments during the hiring process

- Being transparent, open, and honest during meetings

- Providing clear avenues for employees to express their needs, concerns, and other thoughts (and responding in a compassionate and calm manner that facilitates trust)

It is important to consider that creating a WOW workplace requires more than just *modeling* mindfulness; mindfulness must be *embodied* for full and lasting impact. There is a lot of talk in leadership circles around 'modeling behavior', and though what we model is important, what lies beyond that?

Embodiment is when the key principles or values we are trying to convey are more than skin deep. It is where you can begin to push at the forcefield boundary of freedom. Consider the following flow:

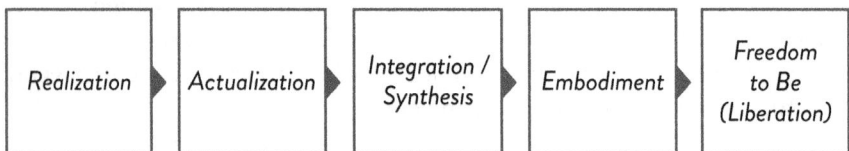

| *Realization* | ▶ | *Actualization* | ▶ | *Integration / Synthesis* | ▶ | *Embodiment* | ▶ | *Freedom to Be (Liberation)* |

It is relatively easy to model mindfulness. This occurs at the level of realization where we have a *conceptual* understanding of why something (let's say compassion) is important. As we begin to deepen our understanding of compassion, we slowly start to integrate it into the fabric of our being. Eventually, we naturally embody it, which helps it to emanate through every word we say and every action we take.

Consider this: 1 out of 10 people are inspired (in a sustainable way) by what you say or tell them. 3 out of 10 people are inspired by the qualities you model. 8 out of 10 people are inspired by what you embody. Embodying mindfulness is therefore a very powerful paradigm of leadership, one that grows and deepens over time.

By embodying mindfulness as leaders in the workplace, we create space for positive emotions to flourish and for the company's mission to deepen and grow. We also strengthen our capacity to address conflicts and challenges and to non-judgmentally and curiously welcome the totality of each employee. Together, engagement, positive emotions, and alignment with a collective mission are what provide us with a sense of meaning and purpose.

And so, consider once more: *What would this type of organization look like? What might be possible if we engage in our workplaces in more mindful ways?* As we commit to this process of discovery, we slowly unveil our company's full and yet always evolving potential (and our own) – moment by mindful moment.

And the ayam™ Experience in My Life

Over the last few years, as a co-founder and Chief Mentor of ayam, I have had the amazing opportunity to be intimately involved in conversations about *well-being at the workplace*. This has led me to have exploratory conversations with organizations aimed at exhorting the virtues of investing in employee well-being on one end, all the way to the opportunity to contribute to the overall thought leadership in this nebulous area by speaking at conferences and writing for top business magazines. And the learning for me has been tremendous and, surprising.

Going into this project, I expected the traditional knowledge industries like tech, etc. to be the fastest adopter of this paradigm. While such organizations obviously exist and I have worked with them, I have been amazed to find a tremendous prevalence and 'promotion' of run-hot culture, in which the employees are literally expected to do "whatever it takes" to meet goals, often at a loss of their personal well-being in most companies, all while the corporate manifestos sing eloquently about the focus on talent and people being the reason d'etre of the business.

Conversely, I expected the traditional manufacturing or bottom-heavy industries to be slower adopters of tech-enabled well-being platforms. Yet surprisingly, many of them have wholeheartedly invested in and adopted this as a corporate priority. In some cases, completely transforming the work culture.

After having been corrected about my assumptions, my inquiry of the what and how has led me to the working conclusion that commitment to workplace well-being has less to do with industry verticals, the size of the business, and profitability, and more to do with the consciousness of the leadership. Each organization where such a rollout has succeeded has the unique feature that their leaders (often the CEO) personally value balance and well-being, model that behavior, and want to make it available to their team members. So, my takeaway has been that the source of the most WOW workplace is a WOW leader, who is, at the very least, a catalyst of this transformation if not the generator!

4

SECTION 4

Moving Forward

The seeds of well-being are many. From gratitude to forgiveness to meaning, purpose, and presence, there is much that goes into feeling alive and aligned with life. At the same time, it does not need to be complicated or overwhelming. All that requires is that we check in with how we're doing right now and consider where we want to go from here.

Well-being begins in the present. It begins here and now. But what is well-being and how can we support it in flourishing? This final section will explore how to step into greater self-care and well-being in everyday life before offering some final points of inquiry to help you bridge that gap between the life you aspire to live and the one you are living now.

CHAPTER 17

Living the Everyday Life: The Paradigm of Self-Care and Well-Being

So, what is our ultimate experience of life? It is the life we are actually living, which is made up of all our small moments. It's our time spent at work (as explored in the last chapter), our time at home, and our time in all the places in between that come together to offer an experience of 'everyday life'. In order to enhance our everyday life experience, we can take a deeper dive into the paradigm of self-care and well-being.

Self-care and well-being go hand-in-hand but the terms are not interchangeable. While both support positive emotions and the unraveling of meaning and purpose, it is helpful to understand the distinction between the two. Where one involves intention and action, the other is an experience of being. Let's take a closer look.

The Distinction and Connection Between Self-Care and Well-Being

We can start this exploration by taking a closer look at self-care. Self-care is what it sounds like – the act of caring for your 'self'. But what is the 'self'? What constitutes it? While we could dive deep into spiritual or philosophical understandings of the sense of self, this is not necessary in order to gain a felt sense of it. Simply speaking, our 'self' constitutes various elements of our experience: our thoughts, feelings, emotions, and sense of vitality and engagement with the world around us. This includes our engagement and relationship with our careers, families, friends, and our sense of meaning or spirituality (to name a few examples).

Self-care, then, is the intentional practice of nurturing all these various dimensions of the self. It is about promoting what feels wholesome and supportive for us and also recognizing what has the opposite effect. In other words, it is about bringing in more of what nurtures us and letting go of what is no longer needed or is toxic to us.

Well-being, on the other hand, is the wellness of our 'being', which begs the question: What is 'being'? Being is the experience of being alive; it is existence. the experience of being alive. We are called human beings and not human bodies for a reason; we are far more than our physical bodies. 'Being' in this human form is the totality of our experience, which includes things like our perceptions, thoughts, actions, and our relationships.

So as a being, where does our experience of being alive arise, and what does it finally come down to? There are many ways that you could answer this question, but what I choose to engage with is the idea that wellness of our whole being is about having a deep sense of meaning, purpose, and engagement in life. Alongside the cultivation of meaning, purpose, and engagement, we experience what this book is fundamentally all about – happiness, joy, and fulfillment.

We could think of self-care as the fuel for well-being. What we put in (and what we let go of) contributes to our experience of wellness and wholesomeness. And as we commit to our well-being (and the practices or actions that support it) we unlock more of our potential. As explored in Chapter 2, we shift from embracing a *'minimum acceptable'* to calling forth our *'maximum achievable'*.

Self-care and well-being are undoubtedly desirable, but why is it so difficult to commit ourselves to them? The answer might rest in our tendency to under-prioritize well-being and to lose our commitment to self-care when life gets busy. This is due to a cognitive bias in that when life 'picks up', we remain committed to our 'tasks' while neglecting our self-care needs. For example, if work becomes more than we can handle, we say "I'm too busy to make lunch. I'll eat out today." We give up what nurtures us rather than what depletes us.

While these trade-offs may be quite justifiable at times, they tend to become a pattern. Rather than addressing why we are too busy or why we don't have the energy for something, we can get into a habit of making trade-offs that ultimately compromise our well-being. Over time, our life becomes full of depleting activities and absent of nurturing ones. This can lead to what psychiatrist and professor Marie Åsberg coined the 'exhaustion funnel'.[86]

The idea of the exhaustion funnel is that as life becomes busier or more stressful, we start to give up more of our lives (more of the nurturing aspects specifically). As nourishing inputs become fewer and farther between, our lives become narrower. First, this might manifest as fatigue, low energy, or sleep problems. As the narrowing continues, we might experience physical challenges, such as hormonal issues, cardiovascular challenges, or chronic pain, all of which impact our mood and mental well-being. And ultimately, this cycle leads us to burnout or exhaustion. Self-care is thus crucial for our experience of wellness.

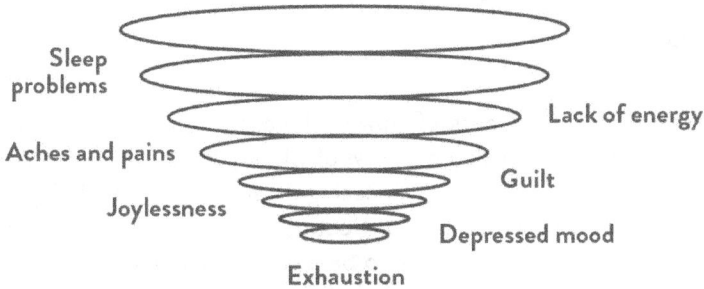

Sleep problems — Lack of energy — Aches and pains — Guilt — Joylessness — Depressed mood — Exhaustion

How to Take Care of Ourselves

Just because self-care is important does not mean we know how to do it. First, what self-care requires is self-awareness. We need to recognize what our needs are in *all* areas of life and we must be aware of how fulfilled these needs are at present. Understanding the concept of the exhaustion funnel can also help us to sense how wide or narrow our life is. Ultimately, we need to ask ourselves: What is the state of my well-being at present? What are my needs?

Once we have taken an honest, non-judgmental, and compassionate look at the current state of our well-being, we can explore two main paths of self-care: intentionally adding more nurturing activities (while letting go of what does not serve us) and shifting from 'tasks and actions' to 'accomplishments and contributions'.

---

86   http://www.mindfulnext.org/burnout-the-exhaustion-funnel/

1. Intentionally Adding Nurturance and Minimizing Depletion

To truly nurture ourselves, we must be willing and committed to making change. This comes from adding what serves us and letting go of what doesn't – at least in small steps. This applies to seven key areas of life:

1. Health and Wellness
2. Family and Intimate Relationships
3. Career and Professional Contribution
4. Social Relationships and Engagement
5. Self-Development
6. Contribution to Society
7. Spiritual Growth

Increasing our awareness of how well we are nurturing each of these domains helps to broaden our view of what it means to 'be well'. Often, we end up with tunnel vision, focusing on success or well-being in just a couple of domains of life while neglecting the rest. How much we nurture these key areas does not have to be perfectly equal and sometimes we simply must go through more depleting times. The intention is not to achieve perfection but to bring balance.

As we aim to bring balance, we not only introduce more of what serves us, but we also might become aware of what we now need to let go. Letting go can be difficult, but it is often a necessary component of achieving balance in our lives. For instance, if we are working 70 hours a week, adding more nurturance is not likely going to be enough. Is there something that also needs to be released or reduced?

It is also worth noting that there are activities in our life that can be both fulfilling and depleting, so there is no easy, one-size-fits-all formula to caring for ourselves. For instance, playing with our children can be deeply nurturing, but it can also deplete our energy. We can become curious about how we can find a balance here. The same goes for caring for a loved one. We do it out of love and compassion, but if we are not caring for ourselves as well, this can lead to fatigue.

2. Shifting From 'Tasks and Actions' to 'Accomplishments and Contributions'

The second step path of self-care offers us the potential to shift not just the content but also the context of our lives (as explored in Chapter 2). Self-care includes nurturing our mindset, and so in shifting from an attitude of 'tasks and actions' to 'accomplishments and contributions', we shift the way we are showing up for our lives. We focus less on the 'what' and more on the 'why'.

This is a crucial act of self-care for times in our lives when the content is not easily or immediately maneuverable. For instance, if we are single parents raising two young children, we might not be able to schedule enough 'me time', but we can certainly focus on how we are relating to what life is asking of us (and making small adjustments to content where possible). However, shifting how we show up for life is not just for times when we have a lot going on. It is a sustainable way of engaging more meaningfully with life no matter what the content of it looks like.

In Chapter 2, I offered examples of how to shift from task-orientation to accomplishment or commitment-orientation. Looking at what we are doing through a contribution lens is also a supportive shift. Consider a few more calendar-entry examples of this:

	From...		To...
10 am	Team meeting (to inform staff of new sales goals and organizational changes).	▶	Meet with team to share our vision of where we see the company going.
3 pm	One-month check-in with Thomas (new sales manager).	▶	Check in with Thomas to see how he's doing and find out how we can support him.
5 pm	Rush the girls to dance practice.	▶	Take my girls to dance so that they can feel joyful, creative, and self-expressive.
8 pm	Make lunch for tomorrow.	▶	Prep a delicious and nutritious meal to nurture myself while at work tomorrow.

As these examples illustrate, the shift from a task lens to an accomplishment or contribution lens is really about focusing on the *why* behind what we are doing. What are we contributing to? What are we accomplishing by bringing care to the small things? This shift unveils the meaning and purpose in our actions and ultimately nourishes our well-being.

Simple Acts of Self-Care for Greater Well-Being

If you are ready and willing to welcome more self-care into your everyday life, there are many simple acts you might consider. What self-care ultimately 'looks like' will be different for each of us; however, the result is the same. Acts of self-care are those that support us mentally, emotionally, physically, and/or spiritually. In each moment, we will require something unique to our needs.

Before I offer a list of examples, it is worth taking the time to tune into one's personal present-moment experience in order to explore what is most needed and/or most nourishing. Take some time to reflect on the following questions, either in mindful contemplation or through journaling.

- Of the seven key areas of life, which areas are yearning for more care or balance?

- What are the needs of these areas? Or, if each of these areas could ask you for one thing, what would it be? Insight might first arise in the form of qualities or energies (i.e. patience, attention) rather than specific actions.

- Then: what simple, everyday acts would honor the needs of the areas in your life that require more balance and care?

- More broadly speaking, what nourishes you? What actions or practices offer you a sense of being nourished?

As we get curious about our experience and the many different realms of our life, we start to uncover the inner whispers that nudge us toward more caring, self-directed action. This mindful self-listening is crucial for cultivating a nourishing everyday life experience.

In addition to any self-care insights that might have come up for you while reflecting on the above questions, you might consider some of the following simple acts of self-care:

- Walking through a natural area

- A coffee break with a friend or partner

- Silently expressing gratitude before meals

- Mindfulness meditation

- Stretching, dancing, or running

- Reading a book that inspires

- Having device-free mornings or evenings

As you consider these self-care practices and any others you might have come up with, take a moment to also consider: What can I commit to for 30 days? Contemplations like the one offered above might leave us inspired, but it is important that we turn this inspiration into action. By setting a goal for yourself that is achievable and specific, it becomes easier to take action on our intention to better nourish ourselves.

Additionally, it is helpful to remind ourselves that we are a multi-faceted human being with many different needs. Grant yourself permission to be a dynamic human with a wide range of needs – including the needs that might typically be difficult for you to honor. Rest and renewal, for instance, are human needs that many of us overlook. Offer yourself the gift of tending to all of your needs. As you do, your capacity to live purposefully, meaningfully, and with full engagement will be enhanced.

Remember, as we explored in Chapter 2, our life is what exists in our calendar. Self-care is not something we do later; we need to make room for it today. As we commit to self-care, our well-being flourishes. Where previously we might have met our 'minimum acceptable', we make space for our 'maximum achievable' to grow. In this way, caring for ourselves is a key ingredient in reaching our full potential. So, since all we ever have is the present, how can you take care of yourself today?

I am that Life is Now

Jen was a high-powered CEO running a business she had built. She felt that she had a perfect life, a good family, a substantial income, a beautiful home, etc. One day, she came home from work and felt unusually tired. She chalked this up to her hectic past few weeks and simply slept early. The next morning when her husband returned from an outstation trip, he woke her up, to her horror, at two in the afternoon. She had overslept by hours and slept through over twenty calls from her work. As she tried to get up she felt a little dizzy, causing her husband to drive her to urgent care. Long story short, in three weeks she had a diagnosis of a brain tumor that was inoperable and probably terminal.

A few weeks later, I happened to meet her after being introduced by a professional colleague. After our initial conversation, she asked me for a private meeting. As soon as we sat down for the session, she immediately started by saying, *"There is so much I have yet to do and experience in life, and it seems like I only have a couple of years left to live. I don't know how to prioritize. Can you help me figure this out?"* I was intrigued by her statement; clearly, she had seemingly made peace with her terminal diagnosis and moved on to trying to get her affairs in order as best she could. We talked for a while, as I gently probed the boundaries of how she was feeling deep down about how her life has suddenly been turned upside down in such a completely unexpected way.

I felt she needed some space to connect with how she was truly feeling, as she still seemed to be in a *'problem-solving mode, albeit this time the end of her life!'* I left her with some inquiries about making a life scorecard to see where she felt she was in life, and what mattered to her most, agreeing to meet her next week.

The following Friday, I got a call from her, asking me if I could somehow see her that day. Sensing the urgency in her voice, I agreed. When she came into my office, she had the unique look of both anticipative anxiety and joy. In her characteristic style, just as she sat down, she started, *"While filling out the life scorecard, I accidentally discovered the source of all my worries and I am now working on solving it. As I was filling in page 2 of things I like to do to nurture myself, it flipped over and rested next to page 1 of what constitutes my day and I was shocked to find that the two pages had nothing in common."*

She went on to share with me how she never realized that she hadn't ever made time for herself while fulfilling all the roles she juggled, and that was now going to be her pursuit and she was really happy!

I was glad to see her happy and wished her well as we parted. I recently met her again, five years after she first met me. Her tumor is in remission, she says, and she has a new design of 30-30-40 life, where 30 is for her company, 30 for family, and 40 for her self-care. She says she has many years to make up for, hence the 40 for self-care!

Hopefully, most of us do not have to wait for a life-altering diagnosis to realize we matter, self-care matters, and that well-being is the foundation of all good things in life!

CHAPTER 18

A Final Inquiry: Who Am I and Where to From Here?

An Expanding Sense of Self

As we reach the closure of this coursebook, the fundamental question we might ask ourselves now is:

Who am I?

If you have arrived at this stage of the book, I imagine that your answer to that question will have shifted since the beginning. As we become curious about things like meaning, purpose, well-being, and personal values, we start to see through old labels that no longer serve us – self-definitions that do not facilitate our growth. When we ask ourselves questions such as those put forth in this book, we often discover that our sense of self grows and shifts. A single sentence or a single question that reaches into some deeper place within us at just the right time has the power to dramatically change things for us.

Furthermore, as we become aware of the journey from happiness and joy to fulfillment and liberation, we become aware of new layers of happiness we have yet to explore. Our capacity for true fulfillment expands as we ourselves do and what we believe possible for this life experience grows. We rest in a wide field of possibilities, trusting that even if we haven't yet experienced it all, there is more to life than what we already know or have felt.

And so, to facilitate your ability to answer that fundamental question, 'Who am I?' take your time to reflect on some of the points of inquiry we explored earlier:

- *What is the content of my calendar?*
- *How do I show up for what's on my calendar?*

- *What do I want more of in my life? Less of?*
- *What seeds of positive emotion am I ready to tend to?*
- *What conversations, relationships, and behaviors do I engage in?*
- *In what areas of my life am I self-expressed?*
- *In what areas of my life am I not self-expressed?*
- *Who am I beneath the labels?*
- *What labels am I willing to give up to be more of who I am?*

As you ponder these questions, consider what has shifted for you. What key insights have arisen during your progression through this coursebook? With so many questions laid out over these chapters, numerous pieces of insight or self-recognition may have come up for you. Take your time to hone in on one, two, or three key insights that have taken root within you since you began this book. What are the most important pieces of insights you have discovered? Notice all of your inner shifts, consolidate them, and in your journal, write down the key things you are walking away with.

The Paradox of Choice: Revisited

All of these questions and the consolidation of key insights lead us to another inquiry, which is:

> ***Who would I now like to create myself as? Where to from here?***

As we explored in Chapter 13, meaning in life is what we make it and, in the same way, we are who we make ourselves to be. Indeed, we all have a unique core self that lives inside of us, but our potential to grow – to expand beyond the limitations we may once have held for ourselves – is ever-present within us. Who we are and what we experience in this life becomes a series of choices.

Now, it is our capacity to choose from a seemingly infinite realm of possibilities that can leave us paralyzed. Choice, as we explored in Chapter 4, is indeed a paradox. On one hand, it offers us more than we could have possibly hoped for and, on the other, too much choice leaves us regretting the choices we do make or are unable to choose at all.

But choosing who we would like to create ourselves to be is not about picking from the pool of choices available in the material world around us. It is not about buying this home or that one or attaining that corporate job or this other one. To choose who we are or who we will become is the act of choosing what might be possible for us; it's not about choosing from what is available to us right now. It is about making the choice to explore who we might become on a deep, meaningful, and purposeful level.

When we choose this path into the unknown – when we choose expansion, conscious meaning, and to unfold our purpose – we shape our actions and decisions based on that. We begin to frame our future – our 'tomorrow' – based on a deeper calling. Our actions slowly transcend achievement and, over time, we unfold self-actualization.

The Blank Canvas of Tomorrow

> *"What we call our destiny is truly our character and that character can be altered. The knowledge that we are responsible for our actions and attitudes does not need to be discouraging, because it also means that we are free to change this destiny."*
> Anaïs Nin

So, where do we go from here? What will we paint of our lives tomorrow? The reality is that from this deep inquiry, you can choose all over again what you want your life to be about. In Chapter two, we took a look at 'real life' and 'the other'. There is the life we are living now and the life we are imagining. How will you bridge the gap between the two to bring more of what you truly long for into your lived reality?

Any label you are willing to give up today is a label that is no longer needed. As you give up definitions and choices that do not serve who you truly are or who you wish to be, you create space for more of what you want to arise and take root. This is what life is about. It is a journey of shedding layers so that we can expand to become all the things we can't even imagine as of yet.

Remember: In every single moment, we are provided with a choice as to how we engage with life. For example, do we choose gratitude or a craving for more in the face of simple gifts? Do we choose rejection or compassion when faced with our human differences? Do we choose to avoid looking inwards or to dive deep (safely, compassionately, and with support as needed) when life challenges us? And, what meaning do we give to each moment? Ultimately, our choices are powerful and our life is crafted by how we choose to paint the blank canvases of today and tomorrow. Life is what we make it.

As a closing note to this section, I will share with you an extract from my favorite childhood book, written by a great author and mathematician (he is known as the father of Set Theory).

Extract from Alice in Wonderland by Lewis Carroll

- Alice: *Would you tell me, please, which way I ought to go from here?*

- The Cheshire Cat: *That depends a good deal on where you want to get to.*

- Alice: *I don't much care where.*

- The Cheshire Cat: *Then it doesn't much matter which way you go.*

- Alice: *...So long as I get somewhere.*

- The Cheshire Cat: *Oh, you're sure to do that, if only you walk long enough.*

Final Thoughts

As we reach the end of this book, consider what chapter of your *life* you are closing and which one you are stepping into. How has what you've learned here shaped your worldview and how will this shift impact your choices? How will you move forward engaging with your environment? How will you express yourself going forward?

Ultimately, there is no 'life' except for the one that we create. The choices we populate our life with are what our life becomes. In this moment and in all those to come, you are faced with choices that can lead you away from who you are destined to become or toward greater meaning, purpose, fulfillment, and ultimately happiness. What choices, then, will you make today and as you step into tomorrow? What beauty – what possibility – will you unfold as you continue through this journey of life?

I will leave you with this question and the final thought, that inquiry allows for insights and a vision to appear. But it's the action we take thereafter that allows for a true embodied and lived experience.

I wish you the best in creating a life you love and that fully expresses you!

www.ingramcontent.com/pod-product-compliance
Lightning Source LLC
Chambersburg PA
CBHW070032100426
42740CB00013B/2669